The Unofficial Collection

## The Encyclopedia of Secret Knowledge about the Famous Video Game Series

Edgar Rommel

Edition 1.1

Author:
Edgar Rommel

Publisher:
Nucleo – a label of
my dna media UG
Ohmstr. 53
60486 Frankfurt am Main – Germany

ISBN:
978-3-98561-037-2

# Hey trainer,

You probably already know Pokémon inside out. It's no surprise the hype around the small and big monsters has not died down after more than 25 years. Pokémon achieved cult status long ago and continues to inspire old fans and young trainers. In this collection of astonishing facts, you will come across all sorts of curious facts about Pokémon that you probably don't know yet.

Apart from fighting and catching Pokémon, there are other areas where Pokémon is making a name for itself. Exciting, funny, and amazing facts about Pokémon are waiting for you in the following pages. Sometimes you will be astonished, sometimes amazed.

Covering more than a quarter of a century of Pokémon history, this book presents the most incredible facts about the Pocket Monsters. Unless otherwise stated, the current data status is September 2022.

And now, have fun catching the curious facts.

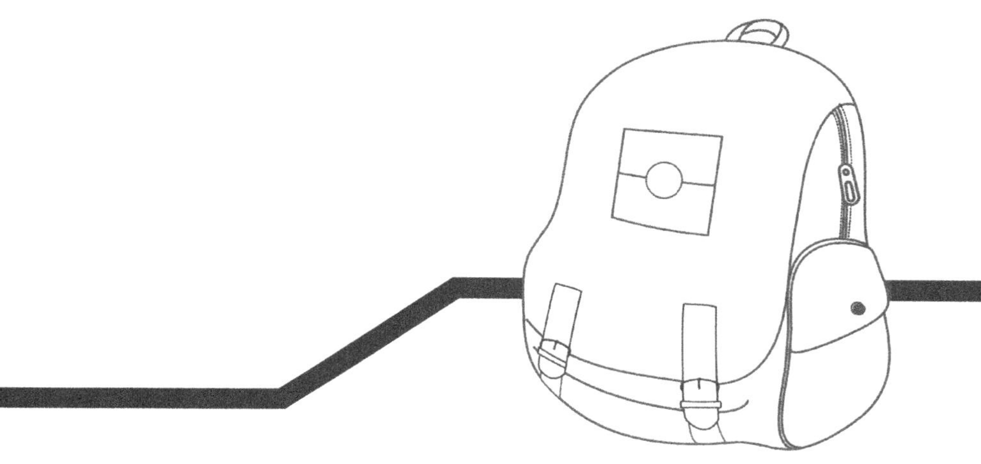

**The first Pokémon ever designed was Rhydon.**

**To honor it, most games have statues at the entrance of the Gyms modeled after the rhino monster.**

## The Adventure Begins

February 27, 1996, marked a milestone in the series when the first Pokémon games for the Game Boy were released in Japan with *Pocket Monsters: Aka* and *Midori* (English: *Pocket Monsters: Red* and *Green*). Just six months later, a revised version with improved sound and graphics and some bug fixes was released in Japan with *Pocket Monsters: Ao* (*Pocket Monsters: Blue*). The first-generation versions of *Pokémon Red* and *Blue* to find their way to the US in the fall of 1998 were based on this updated version. Incidentally, to appeal to Western players, the edition colors red and blue were chosen, as these are the dominant colors in the US flag.

## Town Twinning

The Pokémon world's locations are based on places in the real world. The Kanto region, for example, is modeled after the Japanese region of the same name around the capital Tokyo. Even individual cities are based on existing cities, as is clear from Ecruteak City. Its template is the old Japanese capital Kyoto, known for its historic buildings. Places outside of Japan have also served as the basis for regions. One example is the Kalos region, which is inspired by France.

## Capsules Instead of Balls

Monsters from vending machines is probably the best way to describe the first concept from 1990 that would eventually become Pokémon. Vending machines that dispense capsules with toys inside are widespread in Japan. These capsule machines, called "Gashapon" or "Gatcha," were the initial idea for Poké Balls. But before the Pocket Monsters found themselves in them, they were called "Capsule Monsters" by their inventor Satoshi Tajiri.

Another source of inspiration was the Japanese series *Ultraman*, in which the eponymous hero fights his enemies with the so-called "Capsule Kaiju." "Kaiju" is Japanese for monsters like Godzilla or King Kong. In the *Ultraman* series, these can be summoned from capsules.

Due to legal problems, Tajiri probably changed the name, initially to "CapuMon." Eventually, however, the collectible creatures moved out of their capsules and into their trainers' pockets when they were renamed Pocket Monsters or Pokémon for short.

# Short & Sweet

Over 300 monsters were initially designed for the first Pokémon versions, *Red* and *Green*. Only 151 Pokémon made it into the final version, although some designs were included in subsequent generations.

The Team Rocket trio regularly goes undercover to catch Ash and his friends off guard. Meowth most often disguises itself as the Pokémon Sunflora:
It has chosen this disguise a total of seven times.

A full 87.5 percent of all Combee are male and, therefore, can never evolve as this privilege is reserved for female specimens. Female Combee can be recognized by the lower honeycomb's red feature.

# From Fan Project to Developer Studio

Before Satoshi Tajiri and his friends officially founded the Game Freak development studio and produced video games, *Game Freak* was a completely different project. Under this title, the group of friends founded a gaming magazine that reported on video games beginning in 1983. The illustrations in *Game Freak* magazine came from Ken Sugimori, who later produced the first Pokémon designs. Initially written entirely by hand, the issues were soon professionally printed and sold for 300 yen (about 2.05 dollars).

However, Tajiri became so passionate about video games that he taught himself to code and completed his first game, *Quinty*, in 1987. Two years later, he officially founded Game Freak as a gaming development studio, ending the video game magazine. This was followed by contract work for the Japanese companies Sega and Nintendo. The idea for Pokémon was to be born later.

## Collecting Mania

Even more than 25 years after the birth of the brand, Pokémon records incredible numbers. To date, the anime has been broadcast in 192 countries worldwide. All video games in the franchise combined have sold over 440 million copies. But that's not all: Over 43 billion Pokémon trading cards have been produced.

## Pokémon in its Crawling State

Two kids, two Game Boys, one Game Link Cable – when Pokémon inventor Satoshi Tajiri observed this scene in the spring of 1990, his imagination ran wild. The game developer imagined insects wandering through the cable of the portable video game console. That's how Tajiri, who spent his childhood passionately collecting bugs in the wild, came up with the idea for Pokémon. With this flash of inspiration, he approached the Game Boy developer Nintendo. At first, those responsible there had trouble grasping the concept. Nevertheless, they financed Tajiri and his studio, Game Freak. Additional support was provided by the development studio Creatures, Inc. and by none other than *Super Mario* and *Zelda* creator Shigeru Miyamoto.

## Le Pocket Monster

French mythical creatures? That's probably what one or two parents thought when they first read the name "Pokémon." Where else does the little line above the "e" come from? Since the term is derived from the combination of "Pocket" and "Monsters," people encountered a problem with the abbreviation. In the English-speaking world, "Pokemon" would be read as "Poke Mon" – with a silent "E." This would distort the meaning into "poke monster." Therefore, they used an acute accent on the "E." So, the name "Pokémon" was born, and the monsters stayed in their pockets. Interestingly, this accent is usually used only with foreign words in English (e.g., café), but both "Pocket" and "Monsters" are originally English words.

## Where Am I?

Based on the name of the Pokémon League of the first versions, the Indigo Plateau, some fans assumed that the game world was named after it, but the games never mentioned that the region was called Kanto. However, in the Japanese edition, the player can see a map in the rival's house at the beginning of the adventure that refers to the region as Kanto.

# Flick a Whip

Trainers and Pokémon have a friendly relationship, but in early concepts, the relationship was still rather strained. Originally, trainers would hold ranks. These would be symbolized – similar to martial arts – by differently colored belts. These belts were also supposed to function as whips that trainers used to train their Pocket Monsters. In the end, however, this idea was discarded, and the belts were replaced with badges. The developers at Game Freak chose an "animal-friendly" approach. Nevertheless, some trainer graphics from the first generation hold whips in their hands, such as Team Rocket members and the Gym Leader Sabrina.

## One Step Ahead

Not in first place? That's probably what fifth-generation starter Snivy was wondering about when it looked at the regional Pokédex. Normally, plant starters are ranked first in their respective region's Pokédex. While Snivy is listed as #001 in Unova, it is preceded by the mysterious #000 Pokémon Victini – making it the only monster with that number and the only Pokémon listed before the starters.

## Short & Sweet

The full name of the Pokédex developer is Professor Samuel Oak.

With several new generations, the popular monster Eevee has also received new evolutions. With generation six, only Sylveon was introduced, the only Eevee evolution so far that did not find its way into the Pokémon universe with an alternative evolution form.

Hardly any Pokémon is as slow and, after all, even slow off the mark as a Slowpoke. Perhaps that's why, although it has made numerous appearances in the anime, a Slowpoke has yet to perform an attack in any episode.

## Shiny-Hunters

Among the various forms in which Pokémon can appear, one is particularly coveted. This form – referred to as Shiny – is characterized by its unusual color variation and gleam of light when released from the Poké Ball. Due to the Game Boy's limitations, Shinies were not introduced until the second generation, which was specially optimized for the Game Boy Color's colorful display. At that time, one in 8192 Pokémon was Shiny; however, since the sixth generation, the rate has been halved to one in 4096. So-called Shiny-Hunters are always looking for new methods to increase the chance of a rare find. At 1/99, the chain method using Poké Radar is currently the most promising.

## Pokémon in Pictures

The author Hidenori Kusaka has been responsible for the plot of the Pokémon manga *Pokémon Adventures* since the beginning of the series. The first nine issues were drawn by the illustrator Mato. However, after an illness, she could no longer pursue her work. Her successor was Satoshi Yamamoto.

## Unusual Names

Not Ash Ketchum? That's right, the character of the first Pokémon versions sure has similarities with the anime's protagonist, but his name is different. This is unusual because the character is known as "Red." Adapted from the colors of the first-generation versions, the rival is called "Blue," according to the official canon. While in the first generation, you still play as "Red" from Pallet Town, the character "Red" appears as the final opponent in the games of the second generation *Pokémon Gold*, *Silver*, and *Crystal* and their remakes. "Red" and his rival "Blue" continually appear in other Pokémon series games. "Red" and "Blue" also appear as the protagonist and antagonist in the anime *Pokémon Origins*, whose plot is closely based on the games in the Kanto region. The manga also tells the adventures of the two.

## Like This or Like That?

Some Pokémon can evolve into more than one other monster. A good example is the caterpillar Wurmple, which evolves into a Silcoon or a Cascoon depending on its personality value. However, the record holder is the popular Eevee. It has a total of eight evolutions – so far.

## Gone for a While

Ash Ketchum, the protagonist of the Pokémon anime, grew up with his single mother. At some points, his father is mentioned, but little information about him is available. Thus, like Ash, he is said to be a trainer who started his adventure in Pallet Town. He is said to still be alive. The novel, which was published in Japan in the late 1990s to accompany the anime and written by its writer, Takeshi Shudo, also contains some information. Ash's father is said to have begun his own adventure as a Pokémon trainer immediately after Ash's birth. He has not returned since - probably out of shame since he likely achieved nothing as a trainer.

## From A to Z

One Pokémon but so many different forms: Unown appear in the form of letters, each with an eye. An exclamation mark and a question mark form have also been discovered, so 28 different Unown can be found. Apparently, Professor Oak is also researching other variants. In the third Pokémon movie, his PC shows images of Unown that appear in the form of letters from other alphabets, such as Greek or Cyrillic.

**The city names of each region always follow a specific pattern.**

**In the first-generation Kanto region, all places are named after colors; in Kalos, smells and flavors are the namesake theme.**

# Short & Sweet

*Pokémon Platinum*, an edition of the main series, was released individually in the spring of 2009. It took almost 13 years before another game of the main series was released without a counterpart. *Pokémon Legends: Arceus*, another game of the main series, was released individually in 2022.

Although Mew is considered Mewtwo's predecessor, it comes one spot later in the National Pokédex; Mew is number 151.

If you want to evolve your Inkay, you must turn your Nintendo 3DS device upside down while your monster reaches level 30 – otherwise, the tiny squid won't evolve into Malamar.

## Particularly Special

Every Pokémon has a gleaming form, but not every Shiny is easy to get. Some specific event monsters are not available in Shiny variants – except through cheats. Well-known representatives not appearing as Shinies are the partner Pokémon from the Switch games *Let's Go, Eevee!* and *Let's Go, Pikachu!*.

## A Question of Type

Rock, paper, scissors – this is the battle principle in the Pokémon universe. Certain types have advantages or disadvantages over others. Grass beats Water beats Fire beats Grass. To compensate for some overpowered types, new types were introduced over time. For example, Steel and Dark joined in generation two to balance Psychic. Finally, the Fairy-type was added in generation six, which was meant to weaken Dragon. Thus, there have been a total of 18 types since then. When new types were introduced, some older Pokémon were adapted. For example, starting in the second generation, the floating screw monster Magnemite was given the type Steel besides its first type, Electric. In some cases, types were changed entirely, such as in the sixth generation with Clefairy. It changed completely from Normal to Fairy.

## Come and Catch Them!

"Gotta Catch 'Em All!" This should sound familiar to fans from the beginning. Until around 2003, this was the Pokémon brand's official slogan. However, starting with the third generation of the game series, *Ruby* and *Sapphire*, the phrase disappeared from the game's cover, which has since shown only the version's name.

The slogan was dropped probably because of the sheer number of Pocket Monsters, which increased to an impressive 386 with the third generation's release. Since these are also incompatible with the previous generations, collecting all Pokémon in a single version through official means is no longer possible. However, criticism of the slogan, which supposedly encouraged people to buy all Pokémon products, could also have been a reason for abandoning it. When *Pokémon X* and *Y* were released in 2013, the slogan "Gotta Catch 'Em All!" was reinstated as the brand's motto but no longer appeared on the game covers.

## Trick or Treat

Applin is an unusual lindworm that crawls inside an apple. If you give it a Tart Apple, it evolves into the Grass-Dragon Flapple. If you give it a Sweet Apple, it evolves into Appletun. Although they are entirely different Pokémon, they share the identical Gigantamax form.

## Other Countries, New Forms

Some Pokémon have different forms, depending on their regions of origin. These regional forms can have different types than previously known individuals of the same kind of Pocket Monster. This feature was introduced in early Pokémon anime episodes when Ash and his friends landed on Valencia Island. There, Professor Ivy researched special types of previously known Pocket Monsters. In the games, regional forms were introduced to the seventh generation almost 20 years after the anime version. Since then, over 50 different Pokémon have had regional forms. Only Meowth has two regional forms: Alolan Meowth and Galarian Meowth. The latter can even evolve into a completely different creature – the Steel-type Viking cat, Perrserker – instead of a Persian.

## Deceptive Memory?

Meowth kept claiming to have once been Giovanni's cuddly cat, but apparently, he was nothing more than his servant. After accidentally spilling Giovanni's coffee one day, Meowth was transferred to Jessie and James and, from that day on, completed the Team Rocket trio.

## Calming Environment

Pokémon caught with a Poké Ball are tamed by it. Therefore, they are no longer truly wild. Apart from the pragmatic reason of allowing trainers to carry several Pokémon at once, the invention of the Poké Ball also protected trainers. They no longer had to fear severe injuries from their Pocket Monsters. One Pokémon that was probably responsible for the development of the Poké Ball is the pig-monkey Primeape. Its ferocious temper posed such a danger to trainers that only the technical invention of a taming ball made coexistence possible.

### Shh!

In the N64 game *Hey You, Pikachu!*, the player can shout commands at the little electric mouse via a microphone controller. Rumors quickly spread on the Internet that Pikachu would get mad if you said PlayStation or Sony – Nintendo's fiercest competition at the time of the game's release. In fact, Pikachu understands about 200 words, but neither PlayStation nor Sony triggers a reaction. However, Pikachu does react angrily if you call it an "electric rat."

# Short & Sweet

Although the Team Rocket organization was disbanded after its repeated defeats, the successor syndicate, Team Rainbow Rocket, is forming in the Alola region.

Secret cards are trading cards that are not included in the official listing of an expansion set. An example is the Shining Gyarados from the *Neo Revelation* series, numbered 65/64.

Usually, Pokémon games are released in pairs for the same device. Exceptions are the first *Pokémon Mystery Dungeon* spin-offs. *Red Rescue Team* only appeared for the Game Boy Advance, whereas *Blue Rescue Team* is only available for the Nintendo DS, although they were released simultaneously.

## Prehistoric Pokémon

A Pokémon fossil in the real world? This news went global in January 2017, when paleontologists published their findings of 260 million-year-old fossils. They discovered a new type of prehistoric animal, which they named "Bulbasaurus phylloxyron." Bulbasaurus? Pokémon experts perk up at the name because it's the same as the first Grass-type starter.

So is there a connection here? Not directly. The responsible paleontologists pointed out that fossil finds are usually named after their striking features. Bulbasaurus, for example, is said to have owed its name to its bulbous nose. But the scientists also amusedly admitted that similarities to certain other species might not be entirely coincidental. For example, Bulbasaurus belongs to the genus "phylloxyron," which the scientists translated as "leaf razor," which is, in fact, quite similar to the name for the razor leaf attack, one of Bulbasaur's trademarks. Quite a few coincidences.

# A Personal Secret

Ash's close friend Brock says he has a last name – but he won't reveal it. His English voice actor, Eric Stuart, revealed in an interview in 2006 that Brock's last name is Harrison. Brock's full English name would therefore be Brock Harrison.

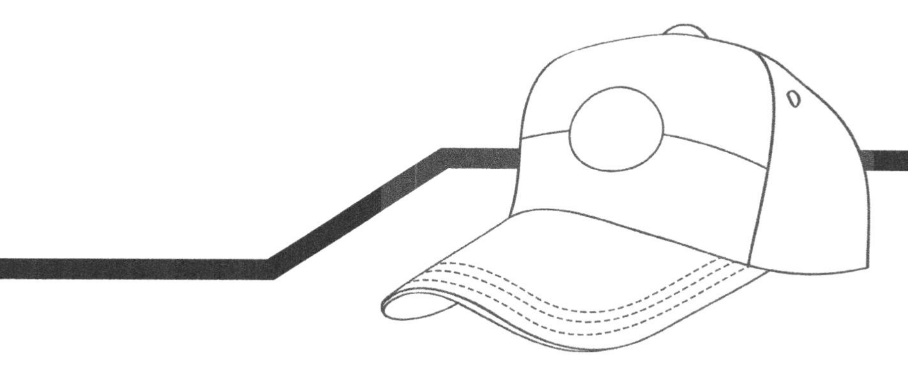

**Not Mickey Mouse, Star Wars, or Hello Kitty – the most successful media franchise in the world is Pokémon.**

**With sales estimated at more than 100 billion dollars annually, no other entertainment brand generates as much revenue from its many products.**

## False Facts

It is commonly accepted that Pokémon creator Satoshi Tajiri has autism, but is this true? The claim comes from the 2009 biography *Satoshi Tajiri, Pokémon Creator* by Lori Mortensen. The author used a MySpace page as a source that allegedly came from Tajiri and featured references to the autism community. So, Mortensen concluded quite simply that Satoshi Tajiri has autism. It did not occur to the author that the page might not have been official. The claim was taken as fact in subsequent years – even renowned media sites and Tajiri's Wikipedia article described his alleged autism. Eventually, an information coordinator from Tajiri's company Game Freak contacted one of these sites and refuted the claim. Satoshi Tajiri has nowhere ever mentioned having autism.

## Boo!

No other type is as special: Ghost is the only type immune to two types at once. Normal and Fighting attacks hit nothing but air. Interestingly, however, Ghost attacks cannot harm Normal-type Pocket Monsters either. Thus, there is a unique mutual resistance.

## Logic Errors

Animals of the real world are repeatedly thematized in the world of Pocket Monsters. Some Pokédex entries mention insects, elephants, or even dinosaurs. And Pikachu is also regularly referred to as an electric mouse – is this an indication that real animals also exist in the Pokémon world? The anime's former head writer, Takeshi Shudo, has a different explanation. According to him, real animals have been extinct in the Pokémon universe for years. The fact that animals occasionally appear in early episodes of the anime is due to inattention by the animation team and a logical error.

## Time for Shopping

In Japan, Pokémon Centers really do exist! You don't get to heal your Pocket Monsters there, but fans can buy various Pokémon items: From stuffed animals to clothes, everyone can find something here. In the Pokémon Center Tokyo DX, the largest store in Japan, there is even the Pokémon Café. If you've always wanted to enjoy milkshakes and sandwiches in the presence of Pikachu and Co, your dream will come true here – assuming you booked early enough, preferably a month in advance.

## Super Smash Pokémon Bros.?

Pikachu! Thunderbolt! On Mario? Such an odd battle has been nothing unusual since *Super Smash Bros.* Gamers worldwide were amazed when Nintendo's unconventional fighting game was released for the N64 console in 1999. The twelve playable characters even include two Pokémon – Pikachu and Jigglypuff. Also included are the Silph Co. rooftop as a battle location and over a dozen Pokémon that can provide support via Poké Ball items. So for the first time, Pokémon could fight not only against each other but other characters as well.

## Sweet Revenge

In the anime, the balloon Pokémon Jigglypuff likes to paint things on other people's faces, but why? Jigglypuff loves to sing, but there is one big drawback: It puts opponents and listeners to sleep. However, this annoys Jigglypuff so much that it scribbles on the sleepyheads' faces. Conveniently, Jigglypuff's microphone is also a felt-tip pen.

# Short & Sweet

The regions of Kanto and Johto are the only areas where a direct connection is known.

Pokémon creator Satoshi Tajiri spent most of his youth in arcades. There, he eventually gambled away so much time and money that an arcade operator gave him a full-fledged *Space Invaders* machine for his home.

Six months before an episode of the anime airs, its production begins. For the Pokémon movies, production begins a year in advance.

*Pokémon Mystery Dungeon: Red Rescue Team* was released in the US in September 2006 and was the last Pokémon game to be released on a Game Boy system.

## Backward

Where is the front, and where is the back? With snakes, you can't always tell at first glance. Looking more closely at the name of the snake Pokémon Ekans, you get "snake" when reading it backward. Its evolution Arbok also has this characteristic, but when read the other way around, the result is "cobra."

## With Good Intention

By now, Fuji-san lives in Lavander Town and cares for orphaned and abandoned Pokémon. Still, his past reveals another facet of him. Not many know that Dr. Fuji lived on Cinnabar Island, where he researched Pokémon with Gym Leader Pyro. The infamous Team Rocket tasked him with creating a clone of the mysterious Mew. After numerous failed attempts, he finally succeeded: The powerful Pokémon Mewtwo was born. However, Dr. Fuji only participated in the project to receive the funds from Team Rocket, with which he hoped to resurrect his deceased daughter through a clone – but he was unsuccessful. Despite his deeds immensely impacting the Pokémon world, Fuji-san is only represented in one trading card.

# More Capacity, More Monsters

Even during the first versions' development, the Game Freak studio repeatedly encountered problems. The relatively inexperienced coders struggled with getting all the data onto a Game Boy cartridge without losing any data, which is why numerous Pocket Monsters had to be deleted in the first generation. However, for the successors, *Pokémon Gold*, *Silver*, and *Crystal*, the goal was more ambitious. The former president of HAL Laboratory and later president of Nintendo, Satoru Iwata, noticed the problems at Game Freak and offered his help. He developed a compression program that created enough capacity for not only 100 new Pokémon but also for a slightly slimmed-down Kanto region complete with eight additional Gym Leaders.

## Do Not Cross the Beams

When a Pokémon is summoned into a Poké Ball, its body dematerializes. When summoned out of the ball, it leaves its energy form and rematerializes into a physical form. Humans are not able to do this. When humans come into contact with a Poké Ball's beam, they are stunned for a short time – but no bad aftereffects are known.

## Smile, Please

At the end of the 1990s, the *Super Smash Bros.* development studio HAL Laboratory was working on a photography game for the N64 console. The developers didn't initially plan for Pokémon to appear in the game. However, the first game concept offered so little motivation that the developers decided to incorporate the popular Pocket Monsters as photo motifs: *Pokémon Snap* was born. The original project name was *Jack and the Beanstalk*, which was probably a reference to the fairy tale of the same name.

## Opposite Extremes

Two criminal organizations are up to mischief in the Hoenn region. While Team Magma wants to increase the land area in the third-generation games and the rival Team Aqua wants to reduce this area, their goals in the remakes of the third generation look a bit more radical. Here, Team Magma wants to increase the land areas so that human civilization can spread further. On the other hand, Team Aqua goes one step further: By destroying all land masses, humanity should also be destroyed, thus enabling a new beginning for Pokémon.

## Cuddly and Cozy

A Pokémon should always feel comfortable. A Poké Ball's interior was designed with this in mind. Pocket Monsters adopt a crouching posture when in danger to recover and protect themselves. Therefore, the balls' interior is designed so the Pokémon would prefer to stay inside at all times and feel protected. But exceptions prove the rule: Ash's Pikachu, for example, prefers to enjoy its freedom outside.

# Short & Sweet

So successful and yet so shy – Pikachu's inventor, Atsuko Nishida, doesn't like to be in the spotlight. For example, she hid her face behind a plush Pikachu in all the picture shots of an official interview from 2018.

Professor Oak's partner Pokémon and the Pocket Monster he trusts the most is Nidorino. This also explains why Nidorino appears mostly in the game intros and Oak's introductions at the start of the game in the Kanto-based versions.

No other Pokémon is as popular with Gym Leaders as Gyarados. Over the first eight generations of the game series, seven Gym Leaders each present their Gyarados.

# When the World Went Crazy

In July 2016, unprecedented hype drove fans and interested people outdoors en masse. The reason: The augmented reality app *Pokémon GO* was released. By August 2016, just one month after its release, five Guinness World Records had already been broken:

1. The highest generated revenue for a mobile game within the first month of release, with 206.5 million dollars.

2. The most downloaded mobile game in its first month, with 130 million downloads.

3. + 4. The top position on mobile game download charts in most countries simultaneously (70 countries) within the first month of release, as measured by download numbers and revenue generated (in 55 countries).

5. The mobile game that generated 100 million dollars the fastest (*Pokémon GO* took just 20 days to do so).

These records are particularly remarkable in light of the fact that *Pokémon GO* did appear later in important markets such as Europe and Japan.

## From Anime to Game

Fans of the Pokémon anime were in an uproar when a yellow edition was waiting for them in stores in 1999. The full name of the Game Boy game is *Pokémon Yellow Version: Special Pikachu Edition*, a revised version of the *Red* and *Blue* editions.

Its storyline and world remain largely the same in the *Yellow* spin-off, but the basic structure has been adapted to the anime. Thus, the player receives a Pikachu at the beginning – just like Ash in the anime – instead of choosing between a Bulbasaur, Charmander, or Squirtle. This Pikachu doesn't stay in its Poké Ball and prefers to follow the protagonist on foot. The infamous Team Rocket trio of Jessie, James, and Meowth make appearances here, as do Officer Jenny and Nurse Joy. In addition, some Pokémon were graphically refreshed, and technical errors were eliminated. Since then, it has been the only game in the main series based on the anime.

## Tough Decision

Multiple save slots or nicknames for the Pocket Monsters – which is more important? The developers of the first Pokémon games had to ask themselves this question because there wasn't enough capacity on the Game Boy cartridge for both. However, since the relationship between the Pocket Monster and the trainer should be the main focus, individualization options such as nicknames were essential for the Pokémon experience – and the decision was not that tough for the developers at Game Freak after all.

## Company Network

Many people think that Pokémon is a Nintendo product and that the Japanese game publisher holds all the rights to it, but this is not entirely true. In April 1998, Nintendo, the Pokémon developer Game Freak, and the licensing company Creatures launched a joint project: The Pokémon Company. Initially intended to manage the Pokémon stores in Japan, the new company quickly became a useful link between the three parties. Since then, The Pokémon Company has taken care of all matters relating to the Pokémon brand in any way – be it games, anime, or merchandise.

## Short & Sweet

The Unova region has a proud 21 cities and other towns – more than any other area to date.

Seven males, one female – in such a ratio appears the Poison-Fire salamander Salandit. The special thing about it: Only the females can evolve into Salazzle.

Every successful boss needs support, and so does Giovanni, the leader of the infamous Team Rocket. He is supported by his secretary Matori, who, since Ash's journey through the Sinnoh region, is becoming more and more prominent and turns out to be Jessie's rival.

Depending on the current season, the appearance of the deer Pokémon Deerling and its evolution, Sawsbuck, changes.

## It's All about the Food

Electric rodent Morpeko generates enormous electrical energy, so it is constantly hungry. That's why it constantly develops a ravenous appetite, which affects Morpeko's appearance and puts the hamster in a miserable mood. Therefore, in the games, its forms change every round.

## Unique Adventures

Each trainer's personal ID number can be found on their trainer pass. It is randomly generated and could have a numeric value of up to 65535 in previous games. In fact, developer Game Freak initially planned to release as many Pokémon game versions. That's right! It was planned that the trainer IDs would affect game elements like environment designs or Pokémon locations, so each player would have a quasi-unique experience based on their ID. However, when *Super Mario* creator Shigeru Miyamoto joined the development team for the first Pokémon games, he ended the ID plans. The concept was too abstract for gamers. Subsequently, they agreed on versions whose game contents differed minimally and were strikingly different visually.

## "That's Right!"

Why can Meowth speak in the anime, while the other Pokémon mostly just say their names? The answer to this question lies in the past. Team Rocket's Meowth lived as a street cat in Hollywood. There, he fell in love with a posh cat named Meowzie, but she rejected the cat, saying she was only interested in humans. This inspired him to learn human language and – unlike other Meowth – walk upright. However, it did not turn out like he wanted with his crush Meowzie: She thought he was a freak. Heartbroken, he joined Team Rocket – because the first word Meowth learned was "rocket."

## Man's Best Friend

James' first Pokémon from his childhood days was a Growlithe named Growlie. He grew up with the Fire dog on the estate of his extremely rich parents, who hardly cared for James. When leaving his parents' home, he left Growlie there, asking it to take good care of his parents. This dramatic backstory ensures that the Team Rocket trio gains a certain sympathy among some viewers and that one would forgive the villains for one or two missteps.

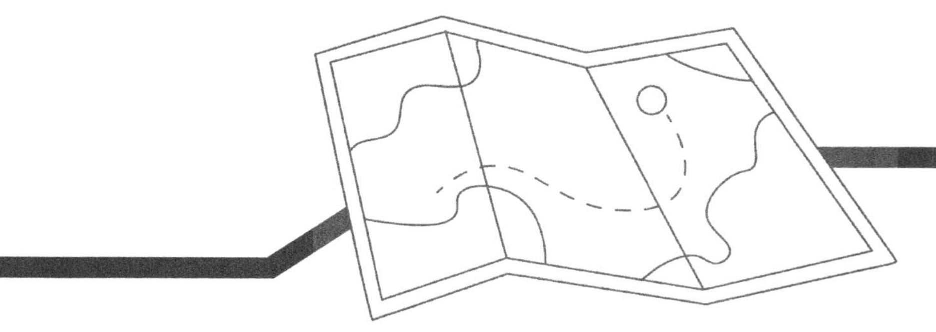

**The size of a Poké Ball can be changed at the touch of a button.**

**At full size, the ball fits perfectly in one hand and is best for throwing, whereas the ping pong ball-like mini size is perfect for carrying and storing one's Poké Balls.**

## On the Big Screen

Most people are probably familiar with *Pokémon Detective Pikachu*, as the movie made big waves with its May 2019 release. But not many know that the cinematic adventure is based on the Nintendo 3DS game called *Detective Pikachu*. It was released in the US a year before the movie. While the stories of the game and the movie are similar, there are still differences. For example, the fate of Pikachu's partner is only revealed in the movie.

## Want a New Name?

In the English test version of the first editions of *Pokémon Red* and *Blue*, some Pocket Monsters had completely different names than in the final version. For example, Jigglypuff and its evolution Wigglytuff were originally called "Pudding" and "Custard." Abra and Kadabra were almost called "Hocus" and "Pocus." The Poison monsters Koffing and Weezing have undergone the most drastic name change. Originally, they were to be called "Ny" and "La" – abbreviations for the American metropolises of New York and Los Angeles.

# Short & Sweet

*Super Smash Bros. Ultimate* was the first of the series that did not introduce a single new Pokémon stage. Seven retro stages were included in the game. Only the Poké Floats stage was not included again.

In some versions, the professors' Pokémon can be a Shiny one in the introductory sequence or in the catch tutorials. Wally can even catch a Shiny Ralts in *Ruby*, *Sapphire*, and *Emerald*, but in future encounters, that same Ralts will no longer be Shiny.

The ninja frog Greninja was announced as a fighter for *Super Smash Bros. for Nintendo 3DS/Wii U* even before *Pokémon X* and *Y*, the sixth generation of games in which Greninja first appeared in the Pokémon universe.

## Short & Sweet

The Shiny Magearna appeared in the anime, but it is not included in the games. Although the eighth-generation games contain data for a Shiny variant of the Pocket Monster, it's the only Pokémon that can't be captured as Shiny.

The Dragon Haxorus was probably the first Pokémon designed in the fifth generation. It was designed before the development of the *Black* and *White* versions had really begun and when Game Freak was still working on *Pokémon Platinum*.

The Pokédex number of boxer Pokémon Hitmonchan is 107, which is exactly how many pounds the protagonist Little Mac of Nintendo's boxing game series *Punch-Out!!* weighs.

# Blastoise, the Wizard

Before the Pokémon trading card game could appear outside Japan, a producer had to be found. Wizards of the Coast, the company responsible for the iconic *Magic The Gathering* trading cards, was chosen as the partner for international distribution. Before The Pokémon Company took over production in 2003, Pokémon cards had been printed by Wizards of the Coast since 1999. To convince the Japanese managers, a few English test prints were made in 1998. For this, the turtle Blastoise had to act as a model: Its pose is already known from the *Blue Version's* cover.

The test prints are unique because a Pocket Monster poses on the front, while the *Magic* card game logo is emblazoned on the back. Only a few cards are known to exist of this rarity. Another Blastoise was made for promotional purposes and featured an unadorned white back. Only two copies of this card were made – while one was sold at auction in the spring of 2021 for about 360,000 dollars, the other Blastoise card remains lost to this day.

## A Nice Tribute

While playing the first Pokémon versions, Japanese gamers might find some familiar names. When choosing names for the protagonist and his rival, the suggested choices include Satoshi and Shigeru. This is a tribute to the Pocket Monster creator Satoshi Tajiri and *Super Mario* founding father Shigeru Miyamoto, who helped developer Game Freak produce the first games. The anime also echoes this tribute: In the Japanese version, the protagonist's name is not Ash but Satoshi, and his rival is Shigeru instead of Gary.

## Not Cool Enough

Each Pokémon belongs to a type, such as Psychic or Electric. Some even have a second type. As of the eighth generation, the least-represented type overall is Ice. With only 51 Pokémon, this type makes up about five percent of all the monsters released so far. The most common type is Water, with 146 representatives, making up about 16 percent of the Pocket Monsters. This includes secondary Ice and Water Pokémon and regional forms. In generation one, Poison Pokémon dominated the tall grass. Since the second generation, players most often encounter Water monsters.

## An Unusual Gift

The monsters in the Pokémon world have the most diverse origins. It's not surprising that some Pokémon were also created by humans. One example is the mysterious monster Magearna, created 500 years ago by a scientist. The sphere inside it is made of Pokémon life energy, which is why Magearna is particularly empathic. The steely gray of its body once consisted of gold, red, and white colors. Magearna takes on this alternate form when it is asleep or tired. It was probably intended as a gift for a princess.

## Pollution

Real-world problems also find their way into the Pokémon universe. This gets obvious while looking at three particular Pocket Monster lines. The evolutionary series of Muk and Koffing represent water and air pollution. The garbage bag monster Garbodor and its precursor symbolize man-made pollution on land. Get the hint?

## No Luck for the Duck

No Pocket Monster comes close to the popularity of the mascot Pikachu. Pikachu was chosen as the title character for the remakes of the first versions, released for the Nintendo Switch in the winter of 2018. However, since two versions of the *Let's Go* spin-offs were planned, a counterpart to the electric mouse was sought-after. Initially, the Water Pokémon Psyduck was considered. However, these plans were discarded since the duck's yellow and beige tones make it slightly similar in style to Pikachu. In the end, those responsible decided on the equally popular Eevee, so the versions were named *Pokémon: Let's Go, Pikachu!* and *Let's Go, Eevee!*.

## Without Mercy

That Team Rocket is a ruthless criminal organization is beyond question. For their goals, they even go over dead bodies: When Rocket members in Lavander Town begin to steal the skulls of helpless Cubone, a Marowak mother stands protectively in front of her child. In the process, she is slain by the bullies; since then, she has haunted the Pokémon Tower as a ghost.

## Pull a Leg

Who would not like to play with the sand castle Pokémon Palossand? Probably those who have checked its Pokédex entry. It says it surrounds its prey with sand and sucks out its life energy. That's why there's a pile of bones under each Palossand.

## Nothing but Rumors

Many fans have noticed that the Bug Pokémon Venonat and Butterfree have great similarities – from the eyes to the skin color to the posture of the hands; however, they are not part of an evolutionary series. Therefore, the rumor has spread that Butterfree was swapped with Venonat's real evolution so Ash would have a cute companion joining him on his adventures. However, this doesn't make sense; for one thing, *Pokémon Red* and *Green's* internal ID numbers suggest that Venonat was independently designed from Butterfree. Moreover, the butterfly was created simultaneously with its predecessors, Metapod and Caterpie. Secondly, the Pokémon anime premiered in April 1997, more than a year after the first games had been released – so it was no longer possible to change evolutions.

## A Good Run

Since the release of the first Pokémon movie in Japan in the summer of 1998, at least one more Pocket Monster movie has been released in Japan every July. The first exception was *Secrets of the Jungle*, which was postponed to December 2020 because of the COVID-19 pandemic. For the same reason, no new Pokémon movies were released in 2021 and 2022.

## Eternal Friendship?

One notable scientist in the Pokémon world is Professor Oak from Pallet Town. In the first-generation versions and their remakes, he sends the player and his rival on a journey to complete the Pokédex for him. But before Oak became a scientist, he was probably a gifted trainer, as Agatha reveals in the smartphone game *Pokémon Masters EX.* The two have been friends since childhood. Agatha is the oldest member of the Elite Four from the Kanto region and specializes in Ghost Pokémon. In their youth, Professor Oak and Agatha often trained together, but he always seemed to emerge victorious. However, Agatha has never forgiven Oak for giving up being a trainer and becoming a scientist to develop the Pokédex. She has felt betrayed and abandoned ever since.

## Short & Sweet

Pokémon designer Ken Sugimori had a pet bird with only one leg when he was a child, which inspired him to create the owl Hoothoot. Although it has two legs, it doesn't usually stand on both simultaneously.

At first, the Ghost-Fire Pokémon Litwick seems harmless, inconspicuous, and cute – but appearances are deceptive. Litwick is a candle whose fire only lights up when it absorbs the life energy of humans or monsters.

The Tamagotchi-like Pokémon Pikachu and its successor don't only exist in the real world: In the Game Boy Color game *Wario Land 3*, a treasure called "Pocket Pet" is hidden. In the Nintendo Game-Cube title *Animal Crossing*, the quest item "Pokémon Pikachu Color" is even mentioned directly by name.

## Divided League

The Indigo Plateau is also known as the Pokémon League and represents the greatest challenge for all trainers of the Kanto and Johto regions, which share a league. The name Indigo Plateau fits this perfectly: All city names in Kanto are derived from colors – indigo is a blue hue – whereas Johto's place names are based on plants, and there is an indigo plant.

## Are the Worlds Connected?

The Pokémon world is not identical to Earth. This is evident from maps and representations in the anime and manga. Pokémon Company executive and Game Freak cofounder Junichi Masuda also revealed this in an interview. Although Earth and the Pokémon world are similar, the inhabitants' values differ greatly. In the Pokémon world, he said, humans and Pocket Monsters work together to make it a better place; this is not possible on our Earth. Still, our planet is repeatedly mentioned in Pokémon. For example, the mysterious Mew is found in a Guyanan jungle in South America, and Silph Co. reportedly has a branch in Russia's no man's land while being headquartered in Saffron City.

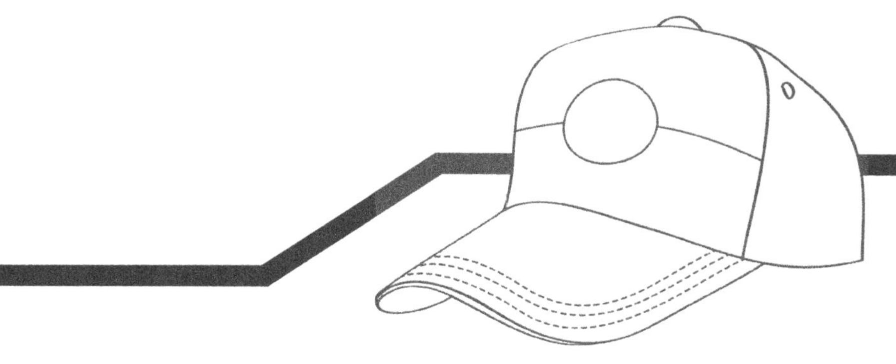

**In June 2022, the 1,200th episode of the Pokémon anime aired in Japan, and even after 25 years running, there seems to be no end in sight.**

**At about 22 minutes per episode, it would take over 440 hours to watch the anime all the way through – that's more than 18 days in a row.**

## Almost Unbeatable

Sableye and Spiritomb are the only Pokémon with the Ghost- and Dark-type combination. This results in them not having any weaknesses until the fifth generation. This disparity was corrected upon introducing the Fairy-type, the sole double damage dealer to Sableye and Spiritomb.

## Chance Missed

In early footage of the safari game *Pokémon Snap*, the snake Ekans appears, but it has been deleted from the final game. This is a pity because the N64 title has only 63 photographable Pokémon.

## Digital and Analog

Following the trading cards' success, the Game Boy Color game *Pokémon Trading Card Game* was released in April 2000. The iconic black cartridge included a limited-edition card: While Japanese players enjoyed an exclusive Dragonite, fans in other countries received a special Meowth. Both cards also appeared in the Game Boy game; Meowth's card was listed as level 14 in the game but was level 13 in physical form.

## Short & Sweet

Mewtwo's origin story was recorded as a radio play and broadcast in Japan in the weeks leading up to the release of the first Pokémon movie. While the recording didn't make it beyond Japan's borders, it was ultimately attached as an animated prequel to the TV special *Mewtwo Strikes Back*.

The Master Ball is guaranteed to catch every Pokémon, making it unique – almost. The Park Ball in Pal Park also has a 100 percent chance, as does the Dream Ball in the fifth-generation Entralink area.

As its name suggests, Hypno specializes in hypnosis. It uses its pendulum to transport people to the land of dreams within three seconds – and then consumes those dreams.

## The Three Wise Monkeys

"See no evil, hear no evil, speak no evil." This Japanese proverb is familiar to most people in the form of three monkeys. One covers its eyes; another, its mouth; and the third, its ears. The three monkeys of the fifth generation of Pokémon – Pansage, Pansear, and Panpour – are based on this proverb. However, the three don't cover their eyes, mouth, or ears. Pansage stands with its mouth open, Pansear even holds its hand to its ear, and Panpour blinks almost demonstratively. Evil!

## Gender Swap

A female can become a male. The baby Pokémon Azurill is the only Pocket Monster that can change its gender after evolving. This was possible until the fifth generation of Pokémon games. The reason for the gender change was simple: Azurill appeared in the wild with a ratio of 75 percent female to 25 percent male. For the evolution of Marill, however, the ratio is 50/50, which ensured that about one-third of all female Azurill became male during evolution. Since the sixth generation, all female Azurill have been allowed to retain their sex after evolution.

## Well Prepared

There are now over 35 types of Poké Balls – everything from Ultra Balls to Premier Balls. Except for generation six, each generation has introduced at least one new kind of Poké Ball that is particularly suited for certain situations. The Net Ball, for example, is very effective with Water and Bug Pokémon, and the Heavy Ball with bulky monsters.

## Art in the Park

When the Pocket Monsters experienced renewed hype thanks to the app *Pokémon GO*, all sorts of memorable things happened in connection with the digital monsters. For example, a few weeks after the smartphone game's release, a five-feet-high statue of Pikachu appeared in a park in New Orleans. An unknown artist seized the opportunity and placed the figure in a neglected fountain overnight. It was made of fiberglass and worked to look like bronze. Embedded in cement near the statue's foundation was the inscription "#pokemonument." In the following weeks, the fiberglass Pikachu fell victim to vandalism before selling at auction in September of that year for about 2,000 dollars. The money went toward constructing a new fountain.

## Appearances Are Deceptive

At first glance, Beautifly looks like a regular butterfly. On closer inspection, however, its pointed proboscis stands out. According to some Pokédex entries, Beautifly thrusts this proboscis into its enemies to suck out their bodily fluids. It is also mentioned several times that it has an aggressive and greedy nature.

## Too Much of a Good Thing

Other countries, other customs – Episode 35 of the Pokémon anime is called *Dratini's Legend* and was aired in Japan in November 1997 without any problem. In most other countries, however, this episode is banned. The main reason for the ban may be firearm use. At the beginning of the episode, a person points the gun barrel in the protagonist Ash's face. This probably went too far.

Most countries did not receive these scenes well, so the entire episode was never aired there. This left a gap in the story because, in the episode, Ash and Brock catch 30 Tauros. Ash takes one of them into his team, and the rest are sent to Professor Oak. So, viewers outside Japan can't understand where Ash got his Tauros from. The episode still holds the record for the most Pokémon captured by a protagonist in one episode.

## Retired Trainer

Researching instead of fighting – Professor Oak has hung up his battle gear for some time. But in the first-generation versions, the player was supposed to be able to fight the scientist. This is proven by trainer data that did not make it into the final game. Due to a programming error, the deleted fight can still be fought. Professor Oak uses five Pokémon: A level 66 Tauros, a level 67 Exeggutor, a level 68 Arcanine, a level 70 Gyarados, and the highest evolution level of a starter Pokémon; a Venusaur, a Charizard, or a Blastoise at level 69. These monsters are partially used by the Pokémon League Champion, so Professor Oak may have even been the intended Champion.

## I Dunno, Audino!

In the Unova region, the pink Pokémon Audino mainly appears in rustling grass and is known for giving players a particularly high number of experience points. Unlike most Pocket Monsters, however, it was not primarily designed for the games but rather with the anime in mind. The Unova region was supposed to introduce new Pokémon, so Audino was supposed to support Nurse Joy, who mainly gets help from Chansey in other areas.

## Short & Sweet

To protect itself from the attacks of its natural enemy, the ant Pokémon Durant has formed a metal armor in the course of evolution, but it's a pity that its biggest enemy is the anteater Heatmor. Heatmor is notorious for its fire attacks and simply melts Durant's steel armor.

In the anime, the Gym Leader Lt. Surge is depicted as one of the tallest people. He is about twice as tall as Ash.

It took five generations of Pokémon for the first pure Flying-only-type Pocket Monster, Tornadus, to appear. All the Flying monsters before had a second different type. Every other type had pure-type representatives before.

## One Trick Pony

Most Pokémon can learn numerous attacks by leveling up or with the help of an attack teacher. However, the letter monster Unown and the transformation Pokémon Ditto are exceptions: Both can learn only one attack. With the help of Transform, Ditto takes on the form of its opponent and can temporarily use some of the opponent's attacks. Unown, on the other hand, is a little different: Except for the attack Hidden Power, it can't perform or learn any other attack.

## Inappropriate

After Jynx made its anime debut on American television in January 2000, a wave of outrage erupted. The Ice Pokémon was said to be a racist stereotype due to its dark skin color, thick lips, and constant hip wiggling. The people responsible reacted to this and changed Jynx's skin color to purple. In addition, some episodes of the anime featuring Jynx have since not aired in the West. The controversy also affected Bellossom, a second-generation flower monster. Initial concept drawings still show it with darker skin, but Game Freak adjusted this and made it green – because Bellossom is inspired by Polynesian dancers.

## Ho ho ho!

Christmas in the Pokémon world? The penguin monster Delibird makes it possible! Its trademark is the attack Present, which, until the sixth generation, was the only one of its attacks that could be learned by leveling up. It always carries presents in a sack. Its appearance - a red body and a distinctive white beard and eyebrows - also resembles the present-distributing Santa Claus. Delibird's presents are a source of great joy, as it is known for bringing food to lost people and those in need.

# When Pikachu Shot with Soccer Balls

Go Pikachu, score a goal! At the *Fifa World Cup* in Brazil 2014, Pikachu supported the Japanese national team as the official mascot. A promotion with German sporting goods manufacturer Adidas unveiled the entire Pokémon soccer team. Of course, the electric mouse received support from ten friends - including its anime rival Meowth. Unfortunately, however, the Pokémon brand's successes did not carry over to the Japanese national team, as they were eliminated from their group in last place, winless.

## Crafting with Pokémon

Pokémon are not only at home on consoles and smartphones. In November 1999, the PC software *Pokémon Project Studio* was released in the US. This application allowed users to design postcards, birthday cards, and other craft items. All 151 Pokémon of the first generation are included as motifs, although some monsters only appear in one of the two released versions.

## Record after Record

With over 154 million units sold, the Nintendo DS is the second-best-selling video game system behind the PlayStation 2. Although *New Super Mario Bros.* precluded a Pokémon game from securing the spot as the best-selling Nintendo DS game with over 30 million copies sold, the title of the fastest-selling game goes to *Pokémon Black* and *White*. In Japan alone, it was pre-ordered more than one million times - a record. Around 2.6 million copies were sold within two days of release - another record. In January 2011, barely four months after release, it broke the five million sales mark. No other Nintendo DS game had previously managed that in such a short time - another record. These records are more impressive when you consider that the versions were released to the rest of the world a few months later.

## Different Worlds of One Universe

Although the games and the anime have probably contributed to each other's success, their characters rarely make follow-up appearances. The anime's protagonist, Ash Ketchum, is mentioned or hinted at occasionally in the games, such as *Pokémon Yellow Version: Special Pikachu Edition*, which uses some elements from the anime. But his actual first and only appearance, in which Ash is also playable, has so far only been in the N64 game *Pokémon Puzzle League*.

## New Recipe

More than 20 years after its initial release, the first Pokémon movie was remade as *Mewtwo Strikes Back – Evolution*. However, the remake is stylistically not a classic anime but uses computer animation and 3D characters. It is the 22nd film in the main series and follows the adventures of Ash and his friends. In the home country of the Pocket Monsters, the remake was released in July 2019, just two months after the premiere of *Detective Pikachu*.

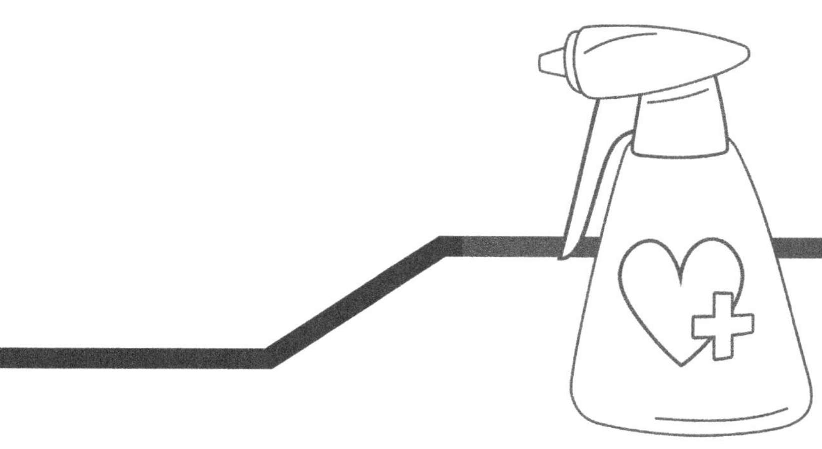

**During the development of the first games, Pokémon Red and Green, only about ten people worked at developer Game Freak.**

**The employees supported each other beyond their areas of responsibility so that, for example, coders also ventured into the designing of Pocket Monsters.**

## The Wrong Pikachu

Pikachu's popularity has inspired the Ghost-Fairy Pokémon Mimikyu to put on a rag modeled after the electric mouse. In this way, Mimikyu hopes to finally make friends. Its true form always remains hidden, and everyone who ever saw it died immediately. Game Freak probably got inspired by the culture of Hawaii and other Pacific islands for the design because Mimikyu's features remind of a mixture of various mythical creatures and ghost stories of that region.

## Weapons Free!

The octopus Octillery and its fish-like predecessor Remoraid look relatively harmless. That a fish would evolve into an octopus, however, seems slightly surprising. However, a look at the early designs of the two second-generation Pokémon reveals that at first, Remoraid was modeled after a revolver and Octillery after a tank. Pokémon officials probably found these designs too morbid, so the monsters' appearances were "toned down." Hints of their original forms can still be found in their names, which include "artillery" and "raid." Moreover, Octillery and Remoraid are assigned to the Pokémon Jet category, which probably references weapons' mechanism. They probably weren't always that harmless, then.

# Short & Sweet

Game Freak co-founder Junichi Masuda's favorite Pokémon is Psyduck. This is not surprising since Masuda's favorite type is Water, and Surfer, his favorite attack.

At the Pokémon Center in New York, there was a real pinball machine in the design of the Game Boy Advance game *Pokémon Pinball Ruby and Sapphire*.

The bird Pokémon Spearow sees the world in shades of gray. This is clear from the first episode of the anime, from a scene in which Spearow's black-and-white vision is revealed.

The Galarian Form of Mr. Mime can evolve into Mr. Rime, but normal Mr. Mime cannot. Regardless of their origin, all Mime Jr. Pokémon in the Galar region evolve into Galarian Mr. Mime.

## A Colorful Line-up

Pokémon presence increasingly expanded in later generations of the *Super Smash Bros.* series. In the GameCube title *Super Smash Bros. Melee*, more Pocket Monsters received an invitation. Pichu and the legendary Mewtwo entered the battlefield.

In *Super Smash Bros. Brawl* for Wii, however, these two had to make room for the fox-like Pocket Monster Lucario and the Pokémon Trainer. However, the latter does not fight himself but instead uses Squirtle, Ivysaur, and Charizard. The Pokémon Trainer's design is based on the protagonist from *Pokémon FireRed* and *LeafGreen*, the first-generation games' remakes.

When *Super Smash Bros. for 3DS/Wii U* was released, the Pokémon Trainer gave way to Charizard, who is now alone. The iconic Mewtwo returned as a downloadable fighter. It was not part of the standard fighter roster. Instead, the frog ninja Greninja debuted.

Four years later, *Super Smash Bros. Ultimate* landed on the Nintendo Switch and promised the ultimate fighting experience - all the fighters that had ever appeared before are returning. Pokémon like Pichu, Squirtle, and Ivysaur are back in the game. The troop is supplemented by the Fire cat Incineroar, so a total of ten Pokémon are playable.

## A Real Asset

The Dragonite trading card included in the Japanese versions of the Game Boy game *Pokémon Trading Card Game* is one of the four legendary cards from the game's story. Thus, it is the only one that also exists as a physical version. The other cards are the legendary birds Articuno, Zapdos, and Moltres. They only exist as digital cards in the game.

## Baa! Baa!

It's no secret some Pokémon are inspired by real-world animals. After a sheep named Dolly was cloned in 1996, Pokémon developer Game Freak created the first drafts for a fitting Pocket Monster. However, these were quickly discarded because the cloned sheep spurred a controversial ethical debate.

## The Mysterious Doll

The Ghost Pokémon Banette appears as a voodoo doll; specifically a toy abandoned or disposed of by its owner. Resentment toward this child drives Banette. However, seeking revenge, someone can stop Bannette by treating it well to dissolve its resentment and the doll's evil spirit.

## From Simple to Difficult

This wasn't there before. With the release of *Pokémon Black Version 2* and *White Version 2*, the games in the main series received a difficulty level for the first time. Using the key system in the Unova Link menu, the Easy and Challenge modes can be activated after the Champion has been defeated. *White Version 2* players will then get the Easy Key, whereas *Black Version 2* players will get the Challenge Key. So to unlock all modes, the keys must be transferred. The difficulty levels differ due to the game's higher or lower artificial intelligence, and the same applies to the levels of the opposing Pokémon used.

### Enjoy Your Meal

Do people actually eat Pokémon? In the world of Pocket Monsters, that's a fair question. There are several references to these special meals. For example, Ash and Brock imagine themselves eating a Magikarp in the anime. Prof. Oak also discusses how he would rather eat his grandson Gary's Krabby than Ash's since it's much bigger and, therefore, tastier. Some Pokédex entries also depict certain Pocket Monsters as tasty treats. Basculin, for example, are considered particularly delicious, whereas Crawdaunt's claws are not recommended.

# Pokémon Stadium Zero?

Pokémon fans were rarely as amazed as in February 2000 when the N64 game *Pokémon Stadium* was released. For the first time, players could fight battles with all 150 monsters in 3D. But was it really the first time?

As is often the case, Japan's fans were prioritized. This is because the game was not only released there a whole year earlier, but strictly speaking, it is the second part of the *Pokémon Stadium* series. The actual first part was released in Japan in August 1998 and was the Pocket Monsters' 3D debut. The game did not make it beyond the Japanese borders.

Its content can be described as a cut-down version of *Pokémon Stadium*. Most game modes are only available when a Game Boy version of Pokémon is connected to the N64. Using Transfer Pak – an add-on for the N64 controller – data from the Game Boy game can be exchanged with the N64. The Battle mode can be accessed independently but offers a meager roster of fighters with only 40 Pocket Monsters. The only Pokémon in the selection that can still evolve is – how could it be otherwise – Pikachu.

## Short & Sweet

Alola reads the same from the front as it does from the back. The name of the island region of the seventh generation is, therefore, a palindrome.

Thousands of years ago, an ancient civilization made the Nazca Lines in a desert in Peru. These lines were drawn into the desert floor that can only be seen from the air. These constellations served as the model for Sygilyph's design – a fifth-generation Psychic-Flying Pokémon.

True to the motto "Gotta Catch 'Em All!" the Spanish police carried out the "Operación Pokémon" in 2012. This uncovered and dismantled a broad-based network of political corruption.

## Make a Wish

With a little patience, dreams can come true. On Route 10 of the Kanto region, there was a picnicker with a special wish. In her opinion, there should be a pink Pokémon with a flower pattern. Numerous years later, this wish came true when the tapir monster Munna found its way into the Pokémon universe with the *Black* and *White* versions. Munna is pink and has a flower pattern on its body like the picnicker had imagined.

## More than a Face

Not all Pokémon are the same. Some Pocket Monsters of the same species can differ from each other. For example, the cobra Arbok has a pattern on its chest that sometimes looks different from specimen to specimen. According to various Pokédex entries, this pattern is supposed to represent a face that Arbok uses to intimidate enemies. While the imitated eyes and mouth have been consistent in games since the fourth generation, previous depictions sometimes differ even within a game generation. In illustrations of the trading cards, the face is not always represented the same, and in the Pokémon manga series, Arbok's chest pattern can change.

## Pokémon instead of Trainer

In the *Pokémon Mystery Dungeon* series, the player slips into the role of a Pocket Monster and explores caves with their team. The first spin-offs, *Red Rescue Team* and *Blue Rescue Team*, were released in the US in September 2006. Almost 14 years later, they were relaunched on Nintendo Switch with *Rescue Team DX*.

## The Original?

The *Pokémon Sword* and *Shield* versions introduced additional regional forms of well-known Pocket Monsters. The Galarian Zigzagoon is one of them. It has a black-and-white color scheme and, unlike the badger monster originally introduced in the Hoenn region, is also a Dark-type. However, according to the Pokédex entry for the *Shield* version, the Galarian form is the original Zigzagoon. Pokémon outside of Galar seemingly lose their Dark-type and take on a brownish coloration like that of the Hoenn Zigzagoon. In addition, their nature becomes more peaceful – Galarian Zigzagoon are notorious for their aggressive behavior. In addition, their evolution Linoone can not evolve outside the regions of *Pokémon Sword* and *Shield* – but in Galar very well grows into a ruthless Obstagoon.

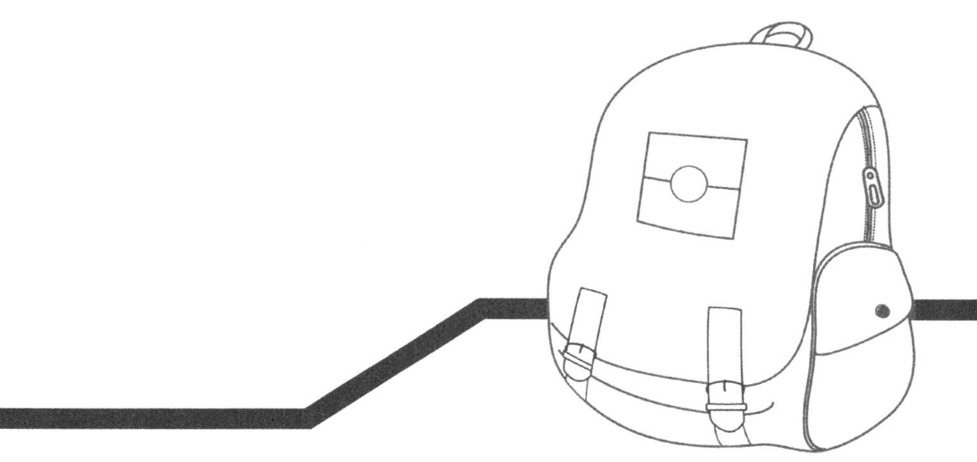

**Clearly, there is a reason behind Eevee's name. The little fan favorite is known for its numerous evolutions – hence, Eevee(lution).**

## Fun at Work

Since the tenth issue, Satoshi Yamato has been the illustrator of the Pokémon manga. In commentary boxes, he uses illustrations of Swalot, which represents him. That's not surprising at all since Swalot is Yamato's favorite Pokémon.

## The Pokémon Shock

Episode 38 of the Pokémon anime's first season, entitled *Computer Warrior Porygon*, or *Electric Soldier Porygon*, achieved a sad fame. After its first broadcast in Japan on December 16, 1997, almost 700 children had to be hospitalized. This was because they suffered epileptic seizures triggered by scenes of strobe light, flickering thunderbolts, and exploding missiles. The Japanese press subsequently dubbed the incident "Pokémon Shock." After clips of the responsible scenes were repeated in news reports, more epileptic seizures occurred. As a result, the episode was never aired again – not even abroad. Moreover, the anime went on a four-month hiatus, and Nintendo's stock price dropped 3.2 percent. The headlines of the shock also reached the US, although the anime's first episode did not air there until nine months later, in September 1998.

## Tight Schedule

More Pocket Monsters had no more room in the first Pokémon games. After the *Red* and *Green* versions went through the final development process, during which all data was checked for errors and corrected, 300 bytes of capacity were laid open. Coder Shigeki Morimoto took advantage of this to secretly code the mysterious Pokémon Mew into the games. This risky maneuver seems unthinkable. But without Morimoto's courage, Mew might never have been created – only two weeks before development finished, he created Mew's design.

## Alien DNA

The mysterious Pokémon Deoxys is not from this world. Instead, it is a virus that reached Earth with a meteorite's help. After a laser beam accidentally came into contact with the alien DNA, the virus formed around a crystal. This is how Deoxys was born. Its form is changeable, and in the third-generation games, it varies from version to version. In later spin-offs, its shape changes depending on its location. Deoxys comes in Attack, Defense, and Speed Formes.

## Just Relax

Even Pokémon need to relax sometimes. Wouldn't it be nice to watch them do so? Or listen to them? The official Japanese YouTube channel makes this possible. Since January 2020, ASMR videos have been periodically uploaded to the channel.

The acronym ASMR stands for "autonomous sensory meridian response" and refers to a phenomenon in which certain sounds or other sensory perceptions trigger a pleasant feeling in the listener. A huge ASMR community has formed online, so it's little wonder that Pokémon executives have recognized the popularity behind the phenomenon.

In one thirty-minute video, for example, you can watch a Charmander enjoy a campfire's crackle. Another ASMR video shows Bulbasaur picking berries, while another clip shows Squirtle before a tropical beach. If you're a fan of Pocket Monsters and delicious food, you'll find a few cooking videos on the official channel. These videos focus mainly on relaxing sounds – and, of course, the Pokémon watching the preparation.

## Like a Scavenger Hunt

There are neither Gyms nor Badges in the Alola region. Instead, the player must pass island trials to be crowned Champion. During this journey, the so-called Trial Captains have tests that are not limited to battles.

## From One to 100

Magikarp, Gyarados, and Regigigas are the only Pokémon that can be caught at level one and 100 in the games. No other wild Pokémon can be encountered at such a low – or high – level. This also makes Regigigas the only legendary Pokémon to appear in the wild at both level one and level 100.

## Printer at Full Speed

Of the more than 43 billion Pokémon trading cards produced to date, nine billion cards were printed in the 2021 business year alone. Normally, The Pokémon Company produces one to two billion trading cards per year, but demand has skyrocketed in recent years. A quarter of all Pokémon cards ever produced were made from 2020 to 2022.

## Echo, Echo, Echo

Necessity is the mother of invention, and due to the limitations of Game Boy, the developers of the first-generation Pokémon games had to come up with a few ideas. As a result, not every Pokémon of the first 151 Pocket Monsters received its own cry. Instead, 37 different sounds were integrated, differing in effects, speed or pitch. However, with two pairs, this trick wasn't used, so Charizard and Rhyhorn share the same cry, and the cries of Poliwag and Ditto cannot be distinguished. With the sixth generation, *Pokémon X* and *Y*, most of the monsters from earlier spin-offs received revised cries – thanks to technology.

## Swarm Intelligence in a Different Way

If you dare to attack the weak fish Pokémon Wishiwashi, you may get the shock of your life. When in danger, Wishiwashi's eyes begin to water and shine, which calls a gathering of fellow Pokémon to its aid. Even Pokémon like Gyarados or Wailord are afraid of this School Form. Judging by its weight, Wishiwashi's School Form consists of 262 individual fish.

## Short & Sweet

Right on top – that's what the graphic artists responsible for designing the English covers of the *Red*, *Yellow*, and *Silver* versions might have thought. On their covers, the Pokémon logo is partially covered by Pikachu's ears, Lugia's or Charizard's head.

In *Super Smash Bros. Ultimate*, the Mii Fighters can be dressed up as Team Rocket members. In fact, this costume is the only one from the Pokémon universe.

The constantly sleeping Pokémon Snorlax always has its eyes closed, even when eating – and Snorlax does little else but sleep and eat. However, if it gets knocked out, Snorlax briefly opens its eyes in shock in most 3D titles of the Pokémon games.

## Really?

In the world of Pokémon, there are several references to real-world events. For example, in the games, a visitor to the Pewter Museum of Science mentions the first moon landing in 1969, and in the anime, May talks about a movie whose plot is reminiscent of the blockbuster *Titanic*.

# Success Despite Frustration

When The Pokémon Company announced the development of the MOBA game *Pokémon Unite* in the summer of 2020, the announcement video quickly became the most disliked video on the company's YouTube channel. There was much criticism of *Pokémon Unite*. It supposedly looked like a cheap *League of Legends* knock-off, the developer TiMi Studio Group was viewed skeptically as part of the controversial Chinese tech company Tencent, and the label as a free-to-play game also made fans mad. The announcement video has since been removed from the channel. After *Pokémon Unite* was finally released for Nintendo Switch and smartphones in the summer of 2021, the criticism did not wear off, especially due to the pay-to-win mechanics. However, this did not dampen its success, as *Pokémon Unite* was downloaded more than 70 million times in the first nine months since its release.

## The Real Pokémon World

Unlike the anime, the plot of the manga *Pokémon Adventures* is somewhat closer to the successful game series. Pokémon executives are thrilled about it; for example, Pocket Monsters creator Satoshi Tajiri said that the manga most closely conveys the world he wanted to share. The president of The Pokémon Company, Tsunekazu Ishihara, naturally wants every fan to read the manga. That's how enthusiastic he is about the story.

## Up the Fins!

Animals behind the wheel – or something like that. Two American students started an unusual project called *Fish Plays Pokémon*. They combined a motion sensor with their aquarium and had their Betta, called Grayson, "play" Pokémon games. Depending on the fish's position in the aquarium, a different button input was activated. Unfortunately, the fish died before the game could be completed. Rest in peace, Grayson!

## A Different Type of Piggyback

In the eighth generation, the Dragon-Ghost Pokémon Dragapult was introduced. As the last evolutionary stage of Dreepy, it carries two Dreepy in pockets on its head. When needed, Dragapult can shoot them at its opponents.

## Teatime

Sinistea and its evolution Polteageist are Ghost Pokémon that settle in porcelain cups and pots. In rare cases, they appear in their original form: Antique cups and mugs, with marks on the bottom to prove their authenticity. The counterfeit forms do not have these marks.

## Difficult to Access

In August 2009, *Pokémon Mystery Dungeon* games were released for home consoles in Japan, for the first time. However, these titles were WiiWare exclusives and could only be downloaded from the Nintendo Wii Shop Channel. In January 2019, the channel was unfortunately closed, so not even Japanese fans can purchase these games anymore.

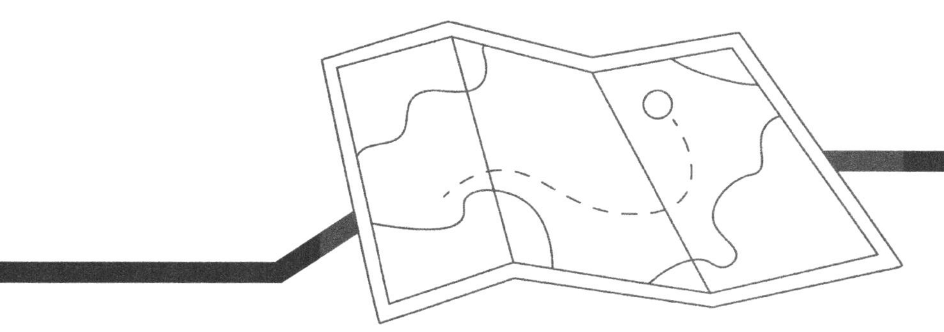

**In November 1999, Pikachu and his friends graced the cover of the prestigious Time magazine.**

**This makes Pokémon the first video game to receive this honor.**

## Short & Sweet

The last Pokémon game released for Nintendo 3DS was *Detective Pikachu* in March 2018.

Which Pocket Monster might be the favorite of The Pokémon Company's president? Since Tsunekazu Ishihara always used the monster Exeggutor for testing during the development of the first versions, *Red* and *Green*, his favorite Pokémon is the many-headed palm tree.

While the Pokémon Tower in Lavender Town was the final resting place for deceased Pocket Monsters in generations one and three, it is transformed into a radio tower in generations two and four.

## A Number Repeats

Pokémon Spiritomb is closely associated with the number 108. According to the Pokédex, the Ghost monster comprises 108 souls banished to the crevice of a stone due to misdeeds. Because it consists of many spirits, it refers to itself in the plural in the *Pokémon Mystery Dungeon* games. Its base defense score is 108, and in the Sinnoh Pokédex – where Spiritomb recorded its first entry – it has the number 108. It can be found in the third-generation *Ruby* and *Sapphire* remakes on Route 108, and Spiritomb weighs – how could it be otherwise – 108 kilograms (238.1 lb). The number alludes to the 108 temptations of life a Buddhist must resist to attain nirvana.

## False Clone

Where the legendary Mewtwo appears, Ditto also live. This is true for Cerulean Cave and Pokémon Mansion on Cinnabar Island, where Mew was once successfully cloned. Therefore, many fans assume Ditto are remains of failed cloning attempts and connected to Mewtwo. When asked about this theory, Pokémon executive Junichi Masuda revealed he had never heard the rumor and that each Pokémon stands for itself with its unique elements. Is that a definite no?

## Where Was Brock?

Some Pokémon fans may have wondered why Brock left Ash and Misty in the Orange Islands adventures, and photographer Tracey took his place. The anime's former executive director and storyboard artist Masamitsu Hidaka revealed why in an interview. At the time, it became apparent that the Pokémon brand would succeed outside Japan, and it was feared that Brock might be perceived as a racist stereotype because of his almond-shaped eyes. Therefore, the European-looking Tracey replaced him. After Brock proved his popularity on the international stage, he returned to the anime.

## Smartphone Meets Pokédex

Who hasn't always wanted to go on a journey with their own Pokédex? Samsung makes this possible – in a way. A Pokémon special edition of the Samsung Galaxy Z Flip smartphone was released in South Korea in April 2022. Included are a carrying case in Pokédex design, protective cases, charms, and other useful accessories. Pre-installed ringtones and wallpapers also convey the Pokémon feeling. Matching Galaxy Buds headphones in a limited Poké Ball design were released a month later.

## Mother and Child

Because Madame Boss, Giovanni's mother, founded the Team Rocket crime syndicate, it could be considered a family business. Her only interest is money, which she prefers to generate by selling Pokémon. She hates the Pocket Monsters and, therefore, doesn't own any. She wanted to dominate the world by capturing Mew and Mewtwo but never succeeded. She lacked a good relationship with her son Giovanni, yet he succeeded her. Contrasting his unscrupulous mother, however, head villain Giovanni at least spoils his companion, Persian, thus seeming almost sympathetic. He can admit defeat in the games as well, albeit unwillingly.

## Green Thumb

Pokémon or watering can? In the world of Pocket Monsters, you sometimes have to look a little closer. Since the second generation, various watering cans based on Pokémon have appeared from time to time in the anime, manga, and games. Thus, there is the Squirt Bottle, the Wailmer Pail, the Sprayduck, and the Sprinklotad. In the games, these items can be used to grow berries.

## The New Son

After Ash's mother, Delia Ketchum, shelters a fugitive Mr. Mime, it moves in with her and helps her with chores. She affectionately calls it Mimey and cares for the Pokémon almost more than for her son. Later in the anime adventure, Mimey becomes part of Ash's team. However, how he catches the Mr. Mime is not shown. It is also the first of Ash's Pokémon to have a nickname, but only Delia addresses it as Mimey.

## Is This Vegan?

In the world of Pokémon, there are some foods made by Pocket Monsters that humans also enjoy. Examples include Miltank Moomoo Milk or the eggs of Chansey and Blissey. These products are probably full of nutrients and are supposed to taste delicious.

## Living Safe

A floating bunch of keys? That can only be Klefki. This Steel-Fairy Pokémon collects keys for fun and even goes as far as stealing them. Guarding its collection like a treasure, Klefki is entrusted with people's most important keys.

## Special Equipment Needed

Alola's islanders sometimes encounter unusual problems. The so-called Ultra Beasts from the Ultra Space get onto the islands through wormholes. Their status as real Pokémon is not 100 percent clear because they are almost impossible to catch with ordinary Poké Balls. Only Beast Balls and Master Balls work on Ultra Beasts. Humans fear them because of their extradimensional skills.

### Big Fish?

Not counting legendary and Dynamax Pokémon, Wailord is the largest of all Pocket Monsters. But at about 47′07″, the whale tips the scales at less than 880 lb of body weight. These extreme proportions led to the rumor that Wailord was lighter than air and could therefore float. Using its 3D model from *Pokémon X* and *Y*, fans tried to calculate the whale's density. The result: The assumption that it was lighter than air could not be confirmed. However, other things contributed to the misunderstanding also. For example, in GameCube's *Pokémon XD: Gale of Darkness*, an old man claims he observed a flying Wailord. The fact that it's also referred to as "Float Whale" is also ambiguous.

## M'lady?

You could describe the fifth-generation starters as noble monsters. As the name suggests, the Grass Pokémon Serperior and its precursors are based on French nobility. The Fire starter Emboar is inspired by a mythological Chinese warrior and the pig of the Asian zodiac. On the other hand, Samurott is based on the Samurai warriors of pre-modern Japan. By representing Japanese, Chinese, and Western history, Pokémon creators wanted to show the Unova region's diverse population.

## Rocket Mother

The ideal Team Rocket member is none other than Jessie's mother, Miyamoto, because she has always faithfully served Giovanni's mother, Madame Boss. She is the first to provide evidence of Mew's existence. She was caught in an avalanche during her expedition to capture the ancient Pokémon for Team Rocket. Initially presumed dead, she has sent reports to Giovanni in subsequent years. She put up her daughter Jessie for adoption so that Miyamoto could save up her money and give it to her daughter later on. This backstory wasn't mentioned in the anime, and Miyamoto never appears there. Instead, this is the main storyline of the radio show *Mewtwo's Birth*, which aired only in Japan.

## Short & Sweet

While the first 260 episodes of the anime were still animated in the conventional cel way – by painting and filming off transparent film – the now standard digital process has been used since episode 261.

With this unique feature, Porygon-Z stands alone: The last stage of the duck series is the only Pokémon with a letter of a foreign alphabet in its Japanese name. The first part of its name is written in Japanese Katakana characters. The Latin letter Z is simply appended.

To celebrate the *Detective Pikachu* movie, you could catch electric mice in detective design in *Pokémon GO*. Those who then evolved their Pikachu could enjoy a Raichu with a detective cap.

## Betta, the Explorer

In October 2020, a Japanese streamer discovered a game bug in the Game Boy Advance title *Pokémon Sapphire* – well, not quite. Instead, his Betta discovered the previously unknown error. The fish activated the key input in an emulator via the position in its aquarium and thus controlled the game character. Somehow, this fish duplicated a rock that should have been moved instead. This made it impossible to advance in the game. The bug hasn't been mentioned in any fan forum or other platforms before, so the Betta is considered the discoverer.

## Vegetarian Dinosaurs

Pokémon for food – there are a few hints of this happening. But over time, such episodes have diminished in number. This is probably because Pocket Monsters are often humanized, and the idea of eating one's Pokémon companion isn't exactly accepted. So it's hardly surprising that some monsters' eating habits have changed. A good example of this is the Flying dinosaur Aerodactyl. In Pokémon's early days, it was depicted as a carnivorous hunter in the anime or Pokédex entries, but in more recent media, it prefers to eat fruit.

## Stronger Together

Playing a single-player game together? The live stream channel *Twitch Plays Pokémon* enables it, and users have even set a world record. Viewers can enter commands in the chat that the avatar executes in the Game Boy game *Pokémon Red Version*. With nearly 1.2 million participants, the project holds the record for "most participants in a single-player online video game." After only 16 days, *Pokémon Red* was completed on March 1, 2014.

## The Last Drop

With the release of *Pokémon Black* and *White,* head designer Ken Sugimori and his colleagues have shared insights into the design of some Pocket Monsters. They also revealed that when it comes to creating the starter Pokémon, the Fire and Grass starters usually don't cause problems – unlike the Water-type. Plenty of ideas exist, but the first drafts mostly look improper and strange. Therefore, the Water starter is usually the last to be completed.

## Hard to Separate

The fish Remoraid and the ray Mantine form a special kind of relationship. They live so close that Mantine was always depicted with a Remoraid under its fin until the game's third generation. This representation was unique; no other Pokémon was depicted with another Pocket Monster. The symbiosis even goes so far that the baby form Mantyke only evolves into a Mantine if a Remoraid is on the team during a level-up.

Slowbro and Slowking also have a special relationship with another Pokémon: Shellder. If the precursor Slowpoke is caught by its tail or head by the shell monster, it evolves into its respective form. However, Shellder's appearance changes so much that it is no longer recognizable. In the Galarian Form, Shellder bites into Slowpoke's arm so that the Galarian Slowbro has an exposed tail but only one free arm.

# Flying Stones

Seymour is a researcher at the Pewter Museum of Science investigating the origin of the Fairy Pokémon Clefairy at Mt. Moon. According to his theory, Clefairy and their evolutionary stages come from outer space. They get to Earth – and sometimes back into space – with the help of spaceships they build from the Moon Stones.

## Miscounted?

The baby Pokémon Togepi has the number 175 in the Pokédex. However, in the DVD menu of the first Pokémon movie, it is listed as number 152. The movie is part of the first generation, which only contains Pokémon up to number 151. Since Togepi belongs to the second generation but already appeared before, it was probably simply numerically adjusted initially.

## Electric Mouse, Right?

Clearly, a mouse! Or is it? Atsuko Nishida designed the series mascot Pikachu in the 1990s. Nowadays, it is also officially called an electric mouse. But Nishida had a different animal in mind when she designed it. At the time, she was, by her admission, in the grip of a downright squirrel boom, which shows in Pikachu's design. Just look at its red cheek pouches and distinctive long tail. Nishida ended up naming the design Pikachu without further ado – "Pika" denotes something electric in Japanese echoism, and she liked "Chu" as a suffix. However, in Japanese, this also refers to the sound that mice make. Chief developer Satoshi Tajiri, therefore, assumed that it must be an electric mouse. This eventually became official canon.

## Short & Sweet

The color and pattern of the eggs Pokémon are hatching from resemble those of the eggs of the Nintendo character Yoshi. This is no coincidence: Pokémon developer Game Freak was responsible for the puzzle game *Mario & Yoshi* before.

On February 6, Mew's clone was born. Its name is Mewtwo.

In the anime, May's little brother, Max, accompanies Ash and his troop on their journey through the Hoenn region. His resemblance to Nintendo's former president Satoru Iwata is no coincidence: Max wears the same glasses as Iwata and was designed in the image of his son.

Designer Mana Ibe invented the flounder monster Stunfisk, the flattest Pokémon.

## The Game That Never Released in Japan

For once, we didn't go empty-handed: The N64 game *Pokémon Puzzle League* was released in the US in September 2000. However, it is unusual that the game was not released in the Pocket Monsters' country of origin, Japan. Years earlier, the game idea, based on the Japanese puzzle series *Panel de Pon*, was given a new look for a Western release on the Super Nintendo and Game Boy by using the *Tetris* license. With *Pokémon Puzzle League*, this puzzle concept was applied to Pokémon. However, it is unknown why the game never made it into Japan's stores.

## From Fruit to Ball

Because of their hard shell, apricorn fruits are perfect to use as Poké Balls. Between 400 and 700 years ago, the first Poké Balls were made from apricorns in the Johto region. Modern Poké Balls do not require fruits to be crafted and were invented about 300 years ago. Nevertheless, even today, specialists like Kurt from Azalea Town work with apricorns.

## Homecoming?

In the Hisui region, Commander Kamado leads the Galaxy Expedition Team. After his home village was destroyed, he wanted to build a new, safe place with Jubilife Village. Where he is from, however, is not mentioned. In the Japanese version of *Pokémon Legends: Arceus*, Kamado occasionally speaks a dialect associated with the Johto region. And in the Italian version of the game, he even mentions places in Johto.

## Fight for Custody

In Grampa Canyon, Ash finds a Pokémon egg that is later stolen by the Team Rocket trio. Meowth lovingly takes care of it at first, but during a scuffle with Ash and his friends, everyone loses track of it, and Togepi hatches from the egg. Afterward, Ash, Brock, Misty, and Meowth have a tournament to see who will be Togepi's trainer. Although Ash wins the mini-tournament, the baby Pokémon Togepi likes to be near Misty most – to the regret of the others. This makes it the only one of Misty's Pokémon that is neither Water-type nor evolves into a Water-type monster – even though that is Misty's specialty.

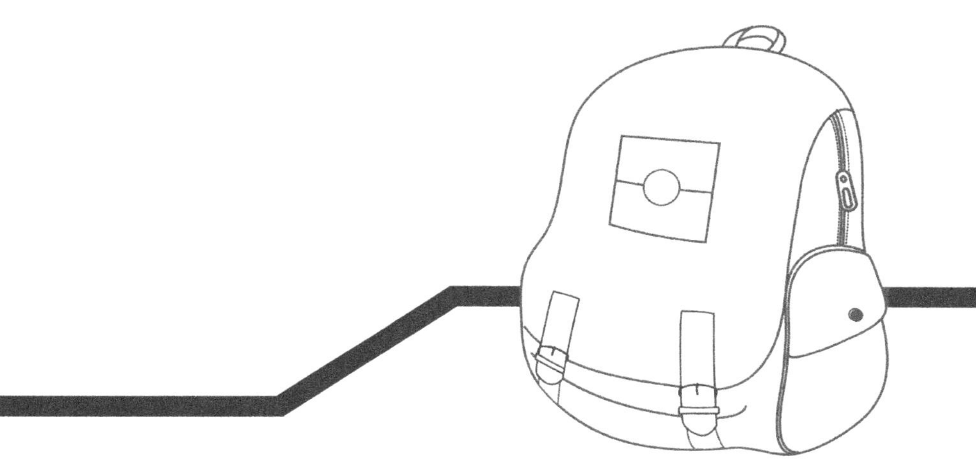

**Every year on February 27, trainers celebrate Pokémon Day because it was on this day in 1996 that the first Pokémon versions were released in Japan.**

## Professor Oak Times Two

In the Alola region lives Professor Samson Oak, the cousin of Professor Oak from Pallet Town. Not only do they look alike, but they are also both active in research. Samson Oak, for example, studies Alola's regional forms in particular. However, one thing distinguishes the two researchers: In the anime, Samson is the first professor to participate in a Pokémon League Conference.

## Number Two

Rock Pokémon and breeding – the Gym Leader of Pewter City, Brock, is an expert in these two subjects. Those who begin their adventure in the Kanto region receive their first Gym Badge from him. Initially, however, Brock was planned to be Gym Leader number two. Concept drawings show an unnamed young trainer who was supposed to be the first leader. He could likely have been challenged in the Viridian City Gym. However, this was switched to Gym number eight, which the player have to conquer last. Afterward, instead of being greeted by a young trainer, Giovanni, the boss of the criminal organization Team Rocket, is awaiting the player.

## Prohibited Zone

You'd think the Pocket Monsters would be popular all over the world. In 2001, however, Saudi Arabia began banning the Pokémon franchise in the country. The country's highest religious authority described the Japanese brand as an advertisement for gambling. Moreover, Pokémon would support Darwin's theory of evolution. As a result, the franchise was banned in most Arab states. Although games and trading cards are now available again in some places, the Pocket Monsters are not particularly popular there.

## A New Battle Mechanic

Have you always felt that the battle mechanics in N64's *Pokémon Stadium* differed from those in the Game Boy games? You're right. The then-developer of the N64 game, Satoru Iwata, didn't receive essential documents from Game Freak. Thus, Iwata had no documentation on Pokémon's fighting mechanics. Instead, he studied the *Pokémon Red* and *Green* duels in such detail that he developed his own fighting mechanics based on them. It took him only a week to incorporate them into *Pokémon Stadium*.

## Long Live the Beaver!

Everyone loves Bidoof! The Pokémon Company has declared the official Bidoof Day to celebrate the little beaver. Since July 1, 2021, trainers worldwide have been celebrating the fourth-generation Pokémon – from events on the smartphone hit *Pokémon GO* to exclusive merchandise. Why July 1 was declared Bidoof Day is unknown, but there are plenty of theories. For example, it is also the national holiday of Canada – and its heraldic animal is a beaver.

## Oven Today, Lawn Mower Tomorrow

What results when "motor" is read backward? Rotom. Machines are getting possessed by the Electric-Ghost Pokémon, which is known to change its form according to whatever device it chooses. In doing so, its secondary type also changes; for example, an occupied refrigerator – a Frost Rotom – features the type combination Electric-Ice. In the anime and the seventh-generation games, Rotom appears as a Pokédex that speaks the language of humans. In the eighth-generation games, it occupies the player's smartphone.

## Short & Sweet

Professor Oak's research must be going pretty well. As he reveals in the Pokémon manga, he has a lab in Pallet Town and a research facility in Cherrygrove City in the Johto region.

Don't lose your head just yet! Porygon-Z and the Ultra Beast Blacephalon are the only two of the more than 900 Pokémon whose heads and bodies are not connected.

From Misty to May and Dawn – Ash's female companion was replaced more than once during his adventures. In an interview, the anime's former executive director and storyboard artist Masamitsu Hidaka jokingly said that this would occasionally give the guys new "eye candy."

## Short & Sweet

Black sheep with white wool – this is the popular Pokémon Wooloo. Interestingly, it has white fur and black wool in its Shiny variant.

The red Gyarados at the Lake of Rage is a Shiny Pokémon. Its color is the result of a forced evolution, in which the precursor Magikarp could not muster enough strength to take on the typical blue of a Gyarados.

Cipher, who in the GameCube games *Pokémon Colosseum* and *XD: Gale of Darkness* corrupt the Pocket Monsters with their dark technology, use physical violence, unlike other criminal organizations in the Pokémon universe. The corrupted Shadow Pokémon also attack people.

# Not Everything Stays the Same

Since the first Pokémon trading cards were released in Japan in October 1996, much has changed in the world – and the same applies to the cards. Over time, their designs have been adapted, and new energy cards have been added to the trading card game. But the backs have remained the same – almost.

The back design of the international trading cards has remained unchanged since their release in 1999. It features two Pokémon logos around an opening Poké Ball that spins in the air and points to the side. The background consists of blue and white swirls of air.

In Japan, in contrast, there are two different back sides. From 1996 to 2002, the cards were adorned with an opening Poké Ball on a dark blue background. The ball was surrounded by golden Pocket Monsters lettering. Since 2002, however, Japan has moved closer to the international design. The two Pokémon logos were adopted, but the Poké Ball faces forward and is surrounded by colored spheres. These colorfully illuminate the blue background. The most striking feature, however, is the gold-colored border of the card. Pretty classy!

## The Monsters No One Knows

What are those weird critters? Users of the Game Boy Camera, released in the US in the summer of 1998, may have wondered this. With the Game Boy Camera, users could take digital photos and decorate them with virtual stickers. The stickers included some images of Pokémon. At that time, however, the Pocket Monsters were still unknown in the US. The first main Pokémon games, *Red Version* and *Blue Version*, weren't released until several months later in the fall of 1998, so it was the Game Boy Camera that brought Pokémon to the US first.

## Super Pokémon Maker

Build your own levels? *Super Mario Maker* makes it possible. But the Wii U game doesn't just let you play as the Italian plumber. For example, if you have a few amiibo figures from the *Super Smash Bros.* series on your shelf, you can scan them. This will unlock the Pokémon Pikachu, Charizard, Greninja, Lucario, Jigglypuff, and Mewtwo as game characters. Those who completed the Pokémon 20th Anniversary Special Days in February 2016 even got to choose a new Pokémon costume. Since the stage was based on Professor Oak's lab, the choices were, of course, Bulbasaur, Squirtle, and Charmander.

## A Different Kind of Fight

From pinball to photo safari, the Pokémon series comes with several curious spin-offs. With *Pokkén Tournament*, the Pocket Monster universe meets the *Tekken* brawlers' game principle. After arcade versions first entered Japanese arcades in July 2015, the game appeared internationally on the Wii U the following spring. Meanwhile, it has been brought to the Nintendo Switch. Over 20 different monsters can compete in one-on-one battles and are accompanied by numerous Support Pokémon.

## An Important Broadcast

In the US, *Pokémon Channel,* a special game, was released for the Nintendo GameCube in winter 2003. The player and his companion Pikachu explore Mintale Town and meet wild Pokémon. They distribute cards that must be collected. The game's highlight, however, is the TV. By watching the various channels, world events can be triggered, and mini-games can be completed. Since *Pokémon Channel* runs in real-time, it takes at least a week to watch all the channels and ultimately unlock the mysterious monster Jirachi.

## Out of Tune

Jigglypuff is not the only Pokémon with arguable singing talent. In the early 2000s, the musical *Pokémon Live!* had performances in countries like the United States, Portugal, and Belgium. It is based on the anime and thus the adventures of Ash Ketchum and his friends. The musical was also supposed to be released as a movie on VHS tape – but the financial success stayed away. Also, critics were not enthusiastic about the performances. Finally, the project was canceled in 2002.

## Give and Take

Every Pokémon trainer probably wants a special gift like this: For The Pokémon Company co-founder Tsunekazu Ishihara's 60th birthday in 2017, employees received a very special trading card. It can be played like a monster card, but Ishihara himself adorns this unusual card. On it, he holds a Master Ball in one hand and a Rotom in the other. With an attack of 1,060, the card will not only make any opponent look like a fool but will let you flip a coin 60 times, and with each "heads," you get to open a gift. A trading card signed by Ishihara reached a price of around 250,000 dollars at an auction in April 2021. Would the coin tosses have been more worthwhile? Unlikely...

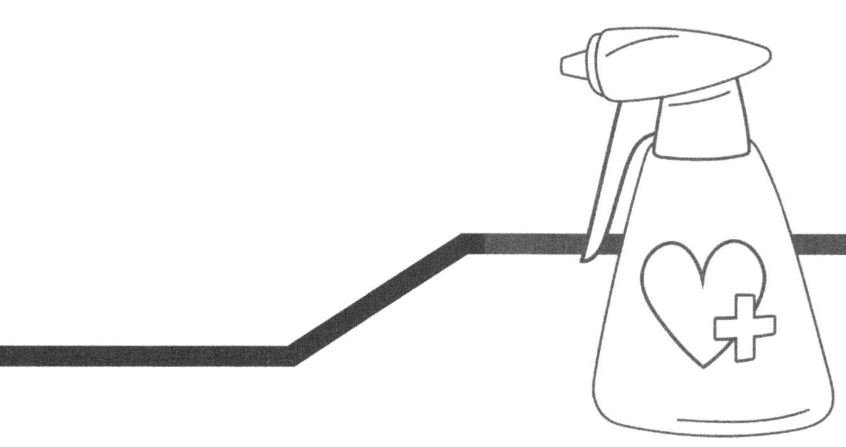

**The place Pallet Town is the starting point of a long journey for trainers like Ash or players of the first generation.**

**In fact, Pallet Town is based on the town of Machida near Tokyo – the hometown of Pokémon creator Satoshi Tajiri.**

## Who Is the Boss Here?

Some legendary Pokémon are ruled over by other beings. For example, the legendary beast trio of Raikou, Entei, and Suicune was revived by the phoenix Ho-Oh after a fire. The legendary titans, on the other hand, were created by the golem Regigigas and can be controlled by him – even when they belong to a trainer.

## On Diet

The shell Pokémon Clamperl can evolve into either a Huntail or a Gorebyss. In the process, it loses quite a bit of body weight. A Clamperl weighs about 115.7 lb, and its evolutions weigh about 59.5 and 49.8 lb, respectively. Even when added together, Huntails and Gorebyss are not as heavy as their predecessors.

## No Familiar Faces Here

*Pokémon Black Version* and *White Versio*n are the first and only games in the main series in which only new Pocket Monsters appear in the regional Pokédex. Only after the Pokémon League is completed do monsters from previous generations appear.

## An Old Legend

The carp Magikarp is always considered one of the weakest Pocket Monsters. But with its evolution, the useless fish becomes the giant Water snake Gyarados. How does this fit together? According to a Chinese legend, a carp that jumps over the dragon gate turns into a dragon. This gate is supposedly located in a waterfall. Guessing, the moral of the story could be that we must first overcome obstacles in order to grow from them. This legend was depicted with Magikarp and its evolution into Gyarados. There are also hints of this story in the *Pokémon Snap* games, for example. Photographers who successfully lure the carp into waterfalls can capture Gyarados afterward – at least with the camera.

## The First Briton...

...who designed Pokémon is James Turner. He worked for developer Game Freak for years, creating monsters like the ice cream cone Vanillite. For the *Pokémon Sword* and *Shield* versions, he was even promoted to lead art designer. Since the Galar region is based on the British Isles, James Turner was just cut out for the role. He has been running his own development studio since June 2022.

## Left in the Dark

While Ash travels through Johto, the mysterious GS Ball initially plays an important role. Professor Oak asked him to bring the ball to the specialist Kurt in Azalea Town. Afterward, however, it was never explained in the anime what the GS Ball was about. From the Pokémon manga, it appears that the ball is made of feathers from the legendary monsters Lugia and Ho-Oh to seal the mysterious Celebi. Since Celebi is the star of the fourth movie, the anime creators didn't want to steal its thunder by revealing everything about the GS Ball in the anime.

## The Zombie Pokémon

The insect Pokémon Paras is an excellent host. It is known for the mushrooms on its back, which begin to grow immediately after birth. These suck the nutrients out of the little bug and grow with Paras. After Paras evolves into Parasect, the mushrooms become fully formed and cover the Pokémon's back. But that's not all. The parasite takes control of Parasect's brain and turns it into its zombie slave – which probably explains its lifeless eyes. The idea behind this comes from nature itself. There is actually a fungus that infects ants. The fungus nests on the ant's body and takes over the insect's actions – just like with Parasect.

## The Meowth Badge

So far in the anime, all the Gym Leaders have been human, right? Not entirely. When Ash wanted to fight Viridian City's Gym Leader, Giovanni was not in his Gym. Instead, he was represented by the Team Rocket trio. This means that not only were Jessie and James once Gym Leaders but that Meowth was as well – the first and only Pokémon to date to take on the role of a Gym Leader.

## Flipping the Ball

In *Pokémon Pinball* for Game Boy Color, the Poké Balls are literally whirled around the game table. Two stages of the *Red* and *Blue* designs are reminiscent of the versions that first appeared in the US. Numerous bonus levels featuring popular monsters such as Gengar or the legendary Mewtwo provide plenty of variety. But why does the game cartridge need a battery? When *Pokémon Pinball* was released in June 1999, it was among the first Game Boy games with a rumble function. *Pokémon Pinball: Ruby and Sapphire*, the successor to *Pokémon Pinball* released four years later, came on a regular Game Boy Advance cartridge and lacked a battery-supported rumble function – the Game Boy Player for the Nintendo GameCube, however, could simulate this directly on the controller.

## Black and White

Normally, Team Rocket members appear in black uniforms. However, the trio of Jessie, James, and Meowth, who are after Ash's Pikachu, are known for their white attire. After being promoted by Rocket boss Giovanni later in the anime, Jessie and James begin to wear black uniforms also. However, this lasts only briefly, as they disappoint Giovanni and are demoted again. They slip back into the white suits and again hunt for Pikachu. Perhaps the black uniforms didn't satisfy the audience since the white outfit has achieved cult status among fans.

## DJ Oak

While Professor Oak is best known in the Kanto region as the creator of the Pokédex, he is mostly recognized in Johto by his voice. In the setting for the second Pokémon generation, he hosts the radio show *Professor Oak's Pokémon Talk* with DJ Mary. Players of the *Gold*, *Silve*r, and *Crystal* versions and the remakes *HeartGold* and *SoulSilver* can receive this show via Pokégear. There, Oak and Mary talk about different Pokémon and where they can be found. In the anime and manga, Mary is considered a star and conducts interviews with famous personalities like Gym Leaders. The show is broadcast from her studio in the Goldenrod City radio tower.

## Short & Sweet

When meteorite Pokémon Minior loses half of its health, it sheds its stone shell and reveals its core. It then glows in one of the seven colors of the rainbow, depending on what kind of dust Minior ate when it entered the atmosphere.

The Gym Leader Lt. Surge was described in early Japanese Pokémon games as a lightning-fast American who served in the US Army. He probably originated in the New York-inspired Unova region, which was at war some time ago and where Lt. Surge also served.

Only the first five Pokémon movies were released in cinemas in the US. From the sixth film on, there was no more distribution on the big screen.

## Harder, Stronger, Better

To create the most powerful Pokémon, Team Plasma reconstructed a fossil, which was then used to create the mysterious insect warrior Genesect. The supposed leader, N, disbanded the project, considering it morally reprehensible. However, one of the scientists continued to work in secret, equipping Genesect with its metal armor.

## Icy Winner

Generation one contains only two Ice-type Pokémon: Jynx and Articuno, making Ice the rarest type in the first versions. Dragon and Ghost share second place with three type representatives each. These include the evolutionary lines of Dratini and Gastly.

## Various Clothes

Burmy is a small, black caterpillar that wraps itself in plants, sand, or trash, depending on the environment. The female evolution Wormadam also wraps herself in a protective cloak. Burmy's male evolution Mothim manages well as an adult moth without such a cover.

## More than Knocked Out

The Pokémon series is suitable for children and outlines a relatively peaceful world, despite its basic concept of monsters fighting each other. The manga turns this image upside down. Here, the battles are depicted in more detail. Pokémon get knocked out and sometimes die. For example, in chapter 14, a Charmeleon cuts the cobra Arbok in two with its claws.

## Bad Mom

The musical *Pokémon Live!* reinterprets the Pokémon story and even has some romantic undertones. For example, Misty's love for Ash is openly addressed, and the story also picks up on the relationships of his mother, Delia Ketchum. In her teenage years, she dated Team Rocket boss Giovanni and belonged to the rogue gang for a while. However, she left Giovanni and Team Rocket for Ash's father. Ash also hinted that Professor Oak and his mother might be in a relationship when he asked him not to bring her home too late. However, this could also reference their actors being in a romantic relationship.

## November is Poké Month

Thanksgiving is celebrated in the USA in November and has a high cultural significance. It is, therefore, unsurprising that November is the peak sales period for consumer goods. This is probably why the Pokémon games of the main series are usually released in November. The USA is an important sales market for the brand. The fact that Christmas is only a month later will also likely increase Pokémon sales.

## The Somewhat Different Lollipop

Slowpoke tails are considered a delicacy in the Pokémon world. The sweet, sappy substance from Slowpoke tails attracts Shellder. When the Shellder bite the tails, they form a symbiotic relationship with the Slowpoke and evolve into Slowbro. Part of the story of the second generation revolves around the evildoings of Team Rocket. The villains steal the tails of the sluggish monsters in the Slowpoke Well and sell them expensively. At first, the tails are still described as sweets that are licked rather than eaten. In later generations, however, some restaurants serve dishes with Slowpoke tails. Especially in the Alola region, Slowpoke tails are a popular ingredient for curry, for example. However, only tails that fall off on their own are used for this – hopefully!

## Better Safe than Sorry

Remakes of old games are not uncommon in the video game cosmos, and the first four Pokémon generations have already been given a new look. Of these, the first-generation versions are the only ones so far that have received two remakes. *Pokémon FireRed* and *LeafGreen* were released for the Game Boy Advance in September 2004, and *Pokémon: Let's Go, Pikachu!* and *Let's Go, Eevee!* were released for the hybrid console Nintendo Switch in November 2018.

## Cute as Always

Each new generation of Pokémon offers one thing guaranteed: Pocket Monsters pretty similar to the mascot Pikachu. They are mainly of the Electric-type, with chubby cheeks, and, above all, they have to be cute. In fact, their primary role is not to be strong but cute. This is what iconic Pokémon designer Ken Sugimori has revealed about the Pikachu clones. Pocket Monsters that will follow in Pikachu's footsteps include Dedenne from the sixth generation of the game. The third generation even got two cute clones, Plusle and Minun.

## The Cursed Town

Lavender Town Syndrome is a legend widely circulated on the Internet. According to this eerie legend, hundreds of Japanese children were driven to suicide after entering Lavender Town in the first versions of *Red* and *Green*. Supposedly, the background music of the town contained binaural beats: Sounds that appear in different frequencies. However, this story is just that – a creepy legend with no truth to it.

## In Search of a Name

People worldwide have heard of Pokémon, but in its origin country, Japan, it has another name. There, the successful brand is also officially marketed as Pocket Monsters. For an international release, however, the abbreviation Pokémon was created. The reason for this is to avoid a legal dispute with the US company Morrison Entertainment Group, which launched the media franchise *Monster in My Pocket* in 1990. The Pokémon managers feared a lawsuit due to the similarity to the name Pocket Monsters, which is common in Japan. And indeed, Morrison sued Nintendo in March 2000 but lost.

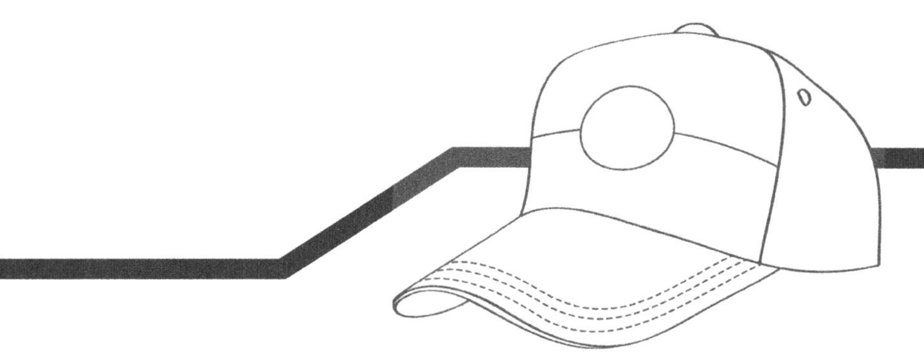

**PokéPark, the first theme park based on a video game franchise, opened its doors in the Japanese city of Nagoya in March 2005.**

**A few months later, however, the unprofitable park was dismantled.**

## Short & Sweet

Although alternate forms of Pokémon have appeared in the anime before, Ash's red-winged Noctowl is the first Shiny monster to make an appearance. No other Shiny appears so often in the anime.

Potions, Poké Balls, and all sorts of useful items – in the Pokémon world, Silph Co. makes all of these products. It's no wonder the infamous Team Rocket occupies the company's headquarters in Saffron City.

The transformation Pokémon Ditto takes the shape of objects or monsters to disguise itself. However, it retains its face – tiny eyes and narrow lips. These features are portrayed, for example, in the anime or trading cards but not in the Pokémon games.

## Everything Remains as it Is

Most, but not all, Pokémon increase in size and weight as they evolve. Ghost Gastly and its next stage, Haunter, weigh only about 0.2 lb. Grimer and its evolutionary stage, Muk, have no weight change; both weigh 66.1 lb. When examining them with the measuring tape, we find more candidates for non-growing Pokémon. The beetle Scatterbug and its successor Spewpa are around 1'00" tall. The gear monster Klang and its evolution Klinklang are double that. And the sword monster Honedge and its successor Doublades are 2'07" tall.

## Different Legendary Forms

Some legendary Pokémon appear in different forms; two examples are the Primal forms of Kyogre and Groudon. The *Isle of Armor* expansion for *Pokémon Sword* and *Shield* was the first to add regional variants of legendary monsters. The bird trio of Articuno, Zapdos, and Moltres received regional Galarian Forms that are not only distinctly different in appearance from the Kanto birds. Their type has also been changed from Ice, Electric, and Fire to Psychic, Fighting, and Dark while retaining the secondary type, Flying.

## From Trios and More

Many legendary Pokémon appear as a trio, a well-known example being the birds Articuno, Zapdos, and Moltres. From the first to the seventh generation, at least one trio has been added with each generation. Some trios have even been expanded over time, such as the legendary titans consisting of Regirock, Regice, and Registeel, joined by Regieleki and Regidrago with the eighth generation.

## Lazy but Powerful

Limited action could be the motto of the sloth Pokémon Slaking. The yeti-like monster is so sluggish that attacking takes ample time. Thus, it can only attack every other turn in the games; in the intermediate rounds, it sits out to lounge. Slaking compensates for this with incredible stats. It has the highest base stats of any non-Mythic, Legendary, or Mega-evolved Pokémon.

## No More Failure

Ash Ketchum does not always have it easy. Especially in fights against Gym Leaders, the anime hero is not always skillful. No wonder he regularly leaves the field a loser and has to ask for a rematch. Only in the anime-exclusive Orange League does Ash defeat every Gym Leader outright. However, fewer challenges await him with only four leaders and the Orange Crew Supreme Gym Leader Drake; most other competitions consist of eight Gym Leaders.

## Worldwide Agreement

Certain Pocket Monsters became the face of the Pokémon brand. The electric mice around Pikachu appear as mascots with each new generation, as do the legendary monsters. Unsurprisingly, The Pokémon Company wants to ensure these essential companions have the same names internationally. It is easier to sell related items when people worldwide recognize Pikachu by name. For "less important" monsters, less attention is paid to internationally similar names. Instead, the creators rely on local translations.

## Working Backward

Which came first, hen or egg? This question can also be asked in the Pokémon universe. Some monster designs were not created in their order of evolution. This was revealed in an interview by Pikachu designer Atsuko Nishida, who was responsible for the appearance of many early Pocket Monsters. For example, she designed the first-generation starters Bulbasaur, Squirtle, and Charmander based on their final evolutions, Venusaur, Blastoise, and Charizard, whose designs had already been determined. Nishida was working backward, so to speak.

## When You Are Hungry

The Water bird Cramorant has an unusual habit. When it dives or surfs, it snaps at other Pokémon. If it has more than half of its Health Points, Cramorant takes the Gulping Form, in which it holds the fish Arrokuda in its beak and can even shoot it at the opponent. However, with less than 50 percent of its health points, Cramorant turns into the Gorging Form, which carries none other than the ever-popular mascot Pikachu in its mouth. And Cramorant can also hurl it at its enemies.

## We Can Save That

Japanese Poké fans are regularly delighted with unusual merchandise. Whether it's sofas shaped like Rowlet or Snorlax, Psyduck teapots, or Gengar pillows whose 66.9-inch-long tongues can be rolled out, in Pokémon's home country, unusual fan merchandise appears often. Fortunately for our wallets, these items rarely get to the US because who can spare several hundred dollars for a Metapod sleeping bag?

## No Road to Glory

Where did the elite go? The Galar region is the setting for the eighth generation and the first region in the main games where the Pokémon League does not consist of the Elite Four. Instead, the Champion is determined in a tournament system. Without an Elite Four, it's also not worth having a victory road that leads to the elite. Thus, Galar is the first region without such a particularly challenging area.

# Mourning Masks

Yamask are Ghost Pokémon that were previously human. They carry around masks of their formerly human faces. Occasionally, they cry when they look at their masks and remember when they were alive. Galarian Yamask, on the other hand, carry around cursed stone tablets. That is why they do not evolve into the sarcophagus Pokémon Cofagrigus but into Runerigus – then the curse of Yamask has completely taken over the lost soul.

## Take That Back!

Did I hear that right? This is a question that players who fought online battles against the Pokémon Chatot during the fourth generation may have asked themselves. Using the Nintendo DS microphone, an alternate cry can be recorded for Chatot's unique attack, Chatter. However, this feature was promptly abused for vulgar exclamations, so Pokémon officials reacted in the following games. In *Black* and *White,* and *Black Version 2* and *White Version 2,* Chatot was banned from online battles. Starting with the sixth generation, the ability to record a custom shout for the parrot Pokémon was removed entirely.

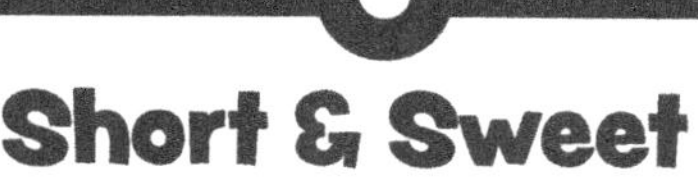

# Short & Sweet

The Fire starter Pokémon of generations three, four, and five begin their journeys as Fire Monsters and then evolve into Fire-Fighting Pokémon: Blaziken, Infernape, and Emboar. This not only represents the most common type of combination of all starters, but it also occurs in three generations in a row.

After participating in developing the *Red* and *Green* versions, Tsunekazu Ishihara came up with the idea for the Pokémon trading card game.

In one scene of Detective Pikachu's screen adventure, the movie *Angels with Filthy Souls* is playing on the TV. It's the same fictional work that Kevin from *Home Alone* watches in some scenes and which was created especially for the Christmas comedy.

## Developing Together

In the spin-off series *Pokémon Ranger* for Nintendo DS, the player takes on the role of a warden primarily concerned with the region's ecological problems. Their role includes catching Pokémon – not with balls, but with the Capture Styler controlled via the handheld's touchpad. A total of three *Pokémon Ranger* parts have been released. The first spin-off was developed by the *Super Smash Bros.* studio HAL Laboratory.

## Where Are the Eggs?

No other monster has such special characteristics as the mysterious Pokémon Manaphy. Apart from Arceus, Manaphy is the only mysterious monster that hatches from a special egg. It can create new eggs through breeding, which have a special appearance. The Water Pokémon Phione hatches from these, but it cannot evolve into Manaphy. They both lack gender, yet Manaphy can be bred exclusively with a Ditto. This makes them the only Pokémon that can be bred but are not available through breeding.

## Fresh Wind

There is always a first time for something, and there certainly are many firsts in the games *Pokémon X* and *Y*. They are the first parts of the main series that do not include "version" in the English titles. They were also both released worldwide as physical versions on the same day, October 12, 2013. That was a first for the main series of Pokémon games and Nintendo games in general. For the first time, *Pokémon X* and *Y* were not followed by a sequel or special versions, as were the *Yellow* and *Crystal* versions in generations one and two, for example.

There were also some firsts in terms of content. For example, the player can use Running Shoes from the beginning to move faster. And the character is no longer bound to a grid but can run around freely in more than four directions. Changing clothes is also possible for the first time. While battles against the Professor were widespread rumors in the schoolyard before, they officially became part of the games for the first time in *Pokémon X* and *Y*. As the first games in the main series with 3D characters, they paved the way for future Pokémon games with numerous innovations.

## Short & Sweet

Only in the Hoenn region can players meet the main character's father – he doesn't appear in any other areas. However, that's not all; the father runs a Gym in Hoenn. Norman awaits your challenge in Petalburg City and specializes in Normal Pokémon.

Gary, Alain, Trip – Ash Ketchum has numerous rivals. However, with no one he has fought as many battles as with Paul from Veilstone City in the Sinnoh region.

The head of the penguin Pokémon Eiscue is enclosed in a block of ice. If it is hit by a physical attack, this block absorbs the damage and exposes Eiscue's head.

## Transposed Numbers?

A mystery that dominated schoolyard conversations in the early 2000s: MissingNo. Anyone surfing the fringes of Cinnabar Island in the *Red* and *Blue* versions may have encountered the cryptic monster MissingNo, which was not an official Pokémon but rather an error in the game. As the name suggests, this game bug has no number and looks like a compressed L formed from jumbled pixels. This is probably due to a bug in the code, which has been corrected in the edited version, *Pokémon Yellow*. This is a pity because the glitch enabled multiplying items; for example, you can never have enough Rare Candy.

## Bad Luck

YouTuber Logan Paul experienced a bitter surprise. In 2021, he spent around 3.5 million dollars on alleged first editions of the basic set of the coveted Pokémon trading cards. Experts were skeptical. Apparently, the boxes looked inauthentic. And the critics were proven right because Paul heeded the clues and opened the sets. To his chagrin, they were filled with *GI Joe* trading cards, not Pokémon cards. Logan Paul took it with humor.

## Pay with Squirtle

Poké Dollars in the real world? The Pacific island nation of Niue makes it possible. There, a special series of one-dollar coins entered circulation in 2001. The emblem of the island state is on one side. If you flip one of these coins over, you'll see a Pokémon. Pikachu, Meowth, Bulbasaur, Charmander, and Squirtle coin the Niue dollar. Popular with collectors, the coins can also be spent like ordinary dollars on the Pacific island.

## Kadabra in Exile

For a long time, there was little news about the Psychic Pokémon Kadabra. The reason is simple: In November 2000, the Israeli mentalist Uri Geller sued Nintendo, claiming that Kadabra was an evil, occult character and an unauthorized parody of him. And parallels can readily be found; Kadabra is just as famous for bending spoons as Geller. In addition, Kadabra's Japanese name, "Yungerer," is derived from Uri Geller. The lawsuit was unsuccessful, but as a result, Nintendo avoided using Kadabra in the trading card game and anime as much as possible. In November 2020, Uri Geller announced that he was reacting to thousands of fan emails that had reached him over the years and explicitly allowed Nintendo to use Kadabra.

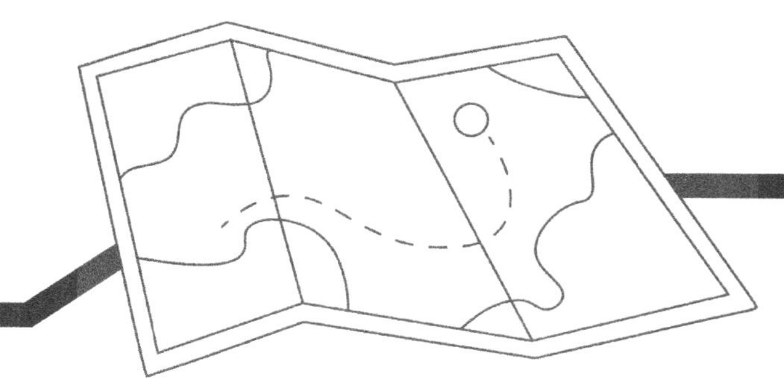

**Arceus is considered a god among Pokémon because it hatched from an egg in the middle of nowhere and created the universe and everything in it with its thousand arms.**

**Interestingly, however, it is never depicted with arms, and, despite its role as a creator, it is not a legendary Pokémon but only a mysterious one.**

## Pikachu on a Diet

Times change – and so do our favorite Pocket Monsters. While Pikachu was still a chubby electric mouse in the 1990s, its design was revised in subsequent releases: Pikachu became leaner. Fans repeatedly accused those responsible of wanting to increase its popularity. But the real reason for the redesign is quite different.

Pikachu was initially developed as a video game character. The Pokémon anime, in which the yellow mouse has a leading role, was created later and took its designs from the games. For the animated series, Pikachu's body had to be adapted to make its movements look more natural. The game designers at Game Freak did not want to preserve Pikachu's old stature. Instead, they wanted to lighten its animation. They decided to define its neck and back more precisely and make Pikachu slimmer. Therefore, its appearance changed over time.

The Gigantamax form that Pikachu can change into in the eighth-generation *Pokémon Sword* and *Shield* games is likely a tribute to the early design of the Pokémon mascot due to its overweight stature.

## Mew as a Truck Driver?

Many fan theories exist about the mysterious Pokémon Mew. Among the most common is that it can be found under a truck in Vermilion City, at the harbor next to the S.S. Anne. This rumor persists because the truck requires detours to reach. Only those who skip sections of the game by trading certain Pokémon can reach the truck – only to discover it is purely cosmetic. No sign of Mew!

## Soul Culture

It seems logical that myths and legends inspired some Pokémon designs. But some designs are not immediately evident to a Western trainer. The Pocket Monsters originated in Japan and contain many references to Japanese folklore. For example, some Pokémon are based on "tsukumogami": Items that become occupied by spirits or souls after 100 years of neglect. One example in the Pokémon world is Voltorb, which resembles a living Poké Ball – its Pokédex number, #100, is undoubtedly a reference to the years of neglect.

## What a Mess

In the US, Lavander Town is located in Kanto and is home to the Pokémon Tower, which serves as the last place of peace for Pocket Monsters. In the German version, the town is called Lavandia – there is also a place with the same name in the French version, but this city is located in the Hoenn region and known in the English version as Mauville City. Mauville is, in turn, the French name for Violet Town in the Johto region. Confusing!

## Queue Up, Please!

Although Pocket Monsters were invented in Japan, the augmented reality app *Pokémon GO* was released there with some delay. Players in New Zealand, Australia, and the US were able to roam the streets and catch digital monsters via smartphone on July 6, 2016. Japanese fans had to wait until the official release on July 22, 2016. Even European trainers could start their adventures a few days before the Japanese. The reason for this unusual procedure was simple: Niantic, the developer behind the app based in San Francisco in the US, did not want to overload its servers with a simultaneous international release. They already had enough to contend with when it came to the rush of trainers.

# Not Just an Empty Shell

The Bug-Ghost Pokémon Shedinja is unique in many ways. For example, it is the only monster with this particular combination. Additionally, no other Pokémon has lower base stats than its pre-evolution. If you train a Nincada to level 20 in the games, carry an empty Poké Ball, and have five or fewer Pokémon on your team, you'll notice something special: Nincada has evolved into a Ninjask and a Shedinja – both Pokémon are now on your team.

That makes sense: Shedinja represents a hatched cicada's cocoon, further explaining its type combination. Ninjask, in turn, is this hatched cicada. However, the cocoon monster's most prominent feature is its number of health points. With only a single health point, Shedinja once again turns out to be an oddball among Pocket Monsters, which means even one hit will put the bug out of action. After all, its ability, Wonder Guard, ensures that it can only be hit by Fire, Flying, Rock, Ghost, and Dark attack types – all other attacks come to nothing. Thus, Shedinja is immune to 13 out of 18 types – another unique selling point in the world of Pokémon.

## Bread Hype

The hype surrounding *Pokémon GO* benefited not only the Pokémon managers. In Japan, for example, the large bakery First Baking Co., which also produces bread in Pocket Monster designs, recorded significant increases in sales. Toy manufacturers also reported record sales, and the anime reached a new peak in viewership.

## Thick and Golden

These special Pikachu cards are not allowed in official tournaments, and the reason for that is simple. For the 20th anniversary of the Pokémon trading card game in 2016, some golden Pikachu cards were produced. That's right, golden! They are made of 24-karat gold and modeled after a first-edition Pikachu trading card. Those who wanted to buy a copy of the gold-plated, chubby electric mouse had to sign up for a lottery first and hope to get lucky. Selected buyers were then allowed to purchase the golden trading card for around 2,000 dollars. The scope of delivery included a frame in which the trading card was embedded for protection. That is certainly a great way to display a golden Pikachu.

## Short & Sweet

No other region can keep up: With a total of 34 routes, the Hoenn region is the record holder.

The first Pokémon game to appear on Nintendo systems, but not published by Nintendo, was the Japan-exclusive Game Boy Color title *Pokémon Card GB2*. The Pokémon Company acted as publisher for the second part of the collectible card adventure.

Team Galactic is wreaking havoc in the Sinnoh region and looking for a lot of trouble. However, unlike other regions' criminal organizations, these crooks are setting the bar high: Team Galactic wants to recreate the entire Pokémon universe, not just the world.

## Short & Sweet

In the anime, Mr. Mime has always had five fingers per hand, but in early designs and the games of the first two generations, it was still depicted with four fingers per hand. Since the Game Boy Advance remakes *FireRed* and *LeafGreen*, however, Mr. Mime has always had a total of ten fingers.

By joining two fossil pieces together in the Galar region, scientists have created the hybrid Pokémon Arctozolt, Dracozolt, Arctovish, and Dracovish. These are the only fossil monsters to date that do not have a Rock-type or gender.

Get well soon! The bones and poisonous fins of the seahorse Seadra are considered valuable ingredients for medicinal remedies.

## Good Night Forever

A lifetime of sleep – for some, it is an unrealizable dream. The koala Pokémon Komala lives this reality. From birth to death, it dozes. The reason for this is the drowsy effect from the leaves it eats. Komala eats or attacks while half asleep. Its trademark is the wooden trunk to which it has clung since birth. Its constant sleep state makes Komala easy prey for the Psychic Pokémon Hypno, which feeds mainly on dreams.

## Additional Stories

Some Pokémon trading cards have beautiful illustrations that can easily tell their story. And some do. From 1999 to 2001, the six-part manga *How I Became a Pokémon Card* by artist Kagemaru Himeno was published in Japan. He tells the background stories for 36 cards he created. The stories are unrelated and feature an illustration of the actual trading card as the climax – a nice idea that unfortunately never made it beyond Japan.

## Bon Appétit!

With most Pokémon, you can see that an animal, mythical creature, or something similar served as inspiration. But what was the inspiration for the gluttonous, ever-tired Snorlax? Or should the question instead be who?

In fact, designer Ken Sugimori modeled the iconic monster after a human. More specifically, his colleague Koji Nishino served as the role model for Snorlax. Nishino has worked as a game designer at Game Freak since the early 1990s. He is known among his work colleagues for eating huge amounts of food, sometimes even spoiled food.

This may also be where Snorlax's Japanese name, "Kabigon," comes from, as the Japanese word for mold is "Kabi." Among his colleagues, Nishino is also known by the nickname Kabigon. Similarities in appearance certainly exist. While some might consider such a Pokémon design an insult, Nishino seemed excited about Snorlax. When asked what his favorite Pocket Monsters are, the burly game designer named Clefairy and Snorlax.

## Show Your Hands!

The renewed hype surrounding Pokémon trading cards during the Covid pandemic took on new proportions in May 2021. After the first attacks in supermarkets became known, the Target chain stopped the sale of all trading cards. In the meantime, competitor Walmart was no longer supplied with new Pokémon cards.

## Better Late Than Never

Before the eighth generation of Pokémon games came out, every type was represented in a Gym – except Dark. With the *Sword* and *Shield* versions, however, this circumstance changed. The Galar region has two Gym Leaders, Marnie and Piers, who specialize in the Dark-type.

## You don't have to count far

Of the more than 900 Pokémon officially released to date, the evolution of the digital duck Porygon is the only Pocket Monster with a numeral in its name: Porygon2. Other Pokémon, like the legendary Mewtwo or the fox Ninetales, also have numbers in their names. However, these are written-out numbers.

## Missing

In the first Pokémon movie, Officer Jenny stops trainers from traveling to New Island due to an approaching heavy storm. However, some trainers do not let this stop them and travel across the rough sea with the help of their Pocket Monsters. Although most of them reach the island, one trainer who flew off on the back of her Fearow is not seen again during the film – she probably never reached the island.

## Essential Goods

During the Covid pandemic, the Pokémon trading card game experienced a second spring. Demand for the cards increased so enormously that some stores had to introduce new policies. Supermarkets in America, for example, limited sales to one booster pack per customer per day. After fans started camping out in front of store entrances overnight, supermarket managers stepped in to stop that, too.

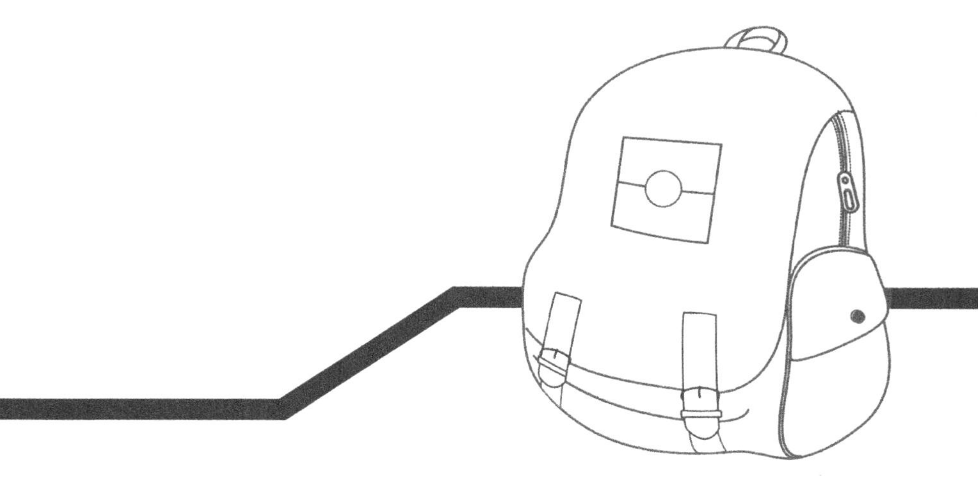

**After more than a thousand anime episodes in over 20 seasons, Ash has finally made it.**

**By winning the tournament in the Alola League, he can finally call himself Pokémon Champion for the first time.**

## What a Risk

Before the first Pokémon games were released for the Game Boy, the project almost had to be scrapped. In the nearly six years before the completion of the *Red* and *Green* versions, developer Game Freak almost ran out of money. When Pokémon creator Satoshi Tajiri told his employees about the financial situation, five of them quit. In the process, he didn't pay himself a salary to not burden the company further. Instead, he lived at his father's expense – a risk that, in retrospect, may have more than paid off.

## Everyone Loves Rainbows

*Mario* and *Zelda* creator Shigeru Miyamoto must think all colors are beautiful. During the production of the first Pokémon games, he suggested developing seven versions – but why seven games, of all things? Miyamoto thought of a rainbow. Each of the seven colors of a rainbow should represent a Pokémon version. In the course of production, however, they eventually planned on two versions. The color selection for these had a special background. Nintendo mascots Mario and Luigi were chosen as color godparents for the Japanese Pokémon *Red* and *Green* versions.

## Ms. Pokémon Universe

For Pokémon Day 2020, The Pokémon Company came up with something special in cooperation with Google: An international poll to determine the most popular Pocket Monster. On February 27, 2020, it became official: With 140,559 votes, the ninja frog Greninja was crowned the winner – followed by Lucario in second place and Mimikyu in third place. A similar poll was conducted the following year, but exclusively via the Japanese Twitter cosmos. And here, the results look different as the Japanese prefer other Pokémon, with Sableye in third place and Cinccino in second; the Electric rodent Dedenne won the race among Japanese trainers with 68,396 votes.

## Many Obstacles

Trainers know that not every Pokémon is easy to find. This became particularly clear in the Game Boy Advance games *Pokémon Ruby*, *Sapphire*, and *Emerald*. On Route 119, Feebas randomly appear on only six of 447 water fields. For the legendary titans Regirock, Regice, and Registeel, players have to take some extra steps and translate and solve puzzles written in the Braille alphabet to reach the titans in the first place.

## Almost Like a Puzzle

The covers of *Pokémon Mystery Dungeon: Red Rescue Team* and *Blue Rescue Team* combined create a scene. While a group of Pocket Monsters on the cover of *Blue Rescue Team* look down a hole in amazement, a troop of Pokémon on the cover of *Red Rescue Team* look up at the said hole in fright. The Nintendo Switch remake *Rescue Team DX* combines these scenes. Its cover features the same monsters in the same location.

## Small but Mighty

A dedicated, handy device just for Pokémon games? That's the Pokémon mini. It was released in the US in November 2001. Half of the 10 official games made it over the ocean – the rest remained Japan-exclusive. The Pokémon mini handheld is the smallest module-based device produced by Nintendo. It's also the Japanese company's first handheld with motion controls and Nintendo's only mobile game console to date to have a vibration function built directly into the console, not only the controllers. In the GameCube title *Pokémon Channel*, some of the Pokémon mini games can be played on the TV. Twenty years later, eager fans are still creating projects that can only be played on the mini device.

# Short & Sweet

Golett and its evolution, Golurk, were created from clay by an ancient civilization. This also explains their type combination of Ground and Ghost.

The starter Pokémon Bulbasaur, Charmander, and Squirtle have one thing in common: They are based on amphibians and reptiles. Bulbasaur's model was a toad, Charmander was designed after lizards, and Squirtle was based on turtles.

No other Pokémon evolves through leveling up as late as Zweilous; only when Zweilous reaches level 64 does it become the three-headed dragon Hydreigon.

## A True Collector's Item

The hype about Pokémon trading cards took on unimagined dimensions in the late 2010s. New sales records are regularly broken – as in February 2022, when a collector reached particularly deep into his pocket at an auction. An Illustrator Pokémon card was auctioned off for a record of around 900,000 dollars.

The card features a Pikachu with a brush. Only 41 copies of the rare item are known to exist worldwide since the trading card was sent only to the winners of a drawing contest of the Japanese magazine *CoroCoro Comic* in 1998.

Its rarity contributed decisively to the sale value, as the condition of the card had been rated as "only" good with a 7/10 score. A few months earlier, an Illustrator Pikachu card with a perfect 10/10 condition changed hands for a record sum of over 5 million dollars. However, YouTuber Logan Paul did not buy the particularly rare trading card at an auction. Still, he bought it privately - and subsequently wore it on a necklace at the Wrestlemania 38 wrestling event.

## More Power

Players of *Pokémon GO* quickly experienced the app really eating up the smartphone battery. To the delight of the battery manufacturers, in the weeks following the initial release, demand for mobile power banks was probably higher than ever before. The share prices of some battery companies rose by up to 25 percent.

## Pikablu

A blue Pikachu? Even before the *Gold* and *Silver* versions were released, a blue mouse regularly appeared in the previews for the second-generation games. Its similarity to the Pokémon mascot Pikachu earned it the nickname Pikablu. Only later did its official name become known: Marill. Ironically, it wasn't blue but pink in the first designs.

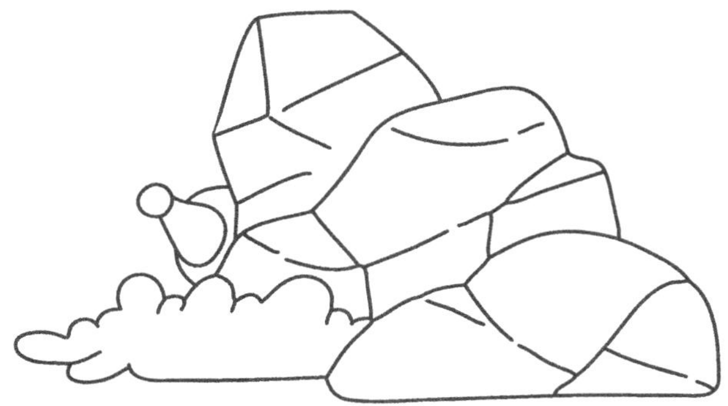

## Exclusive Or for All?

Why does Pokémon software exist for non-Nintendo devices like PCs or smartphones? Many believe the brand belongs solely to the Japanese company, but this is false. The Pokémon Company is only one-third owned by Nintendo, meaning the tech giant cannot solely control the rights to the Pocket Monsters, so a few programs and games are available on other platforms.

## Ticking Save Bomb

Are you worried about your savestates? In the days of Game Boy cartridges, players had to worry about losing their game progress. A little battery inside the cartridge stores the saved information. Once the battery drains, your progress is lost. It usually lasts only a few years. However, the second-generation versions, *Pokémon Gold*, *Silver*, and *Crystal*, drain faster than other main Pokémon games. The reason is simple: The second generation features an internal clock. This can be set in the game and enables day-night changes or events on certain days of the week. This means that the battery is constantly used for tracking time, so it also drains faster.

## Wiggle Wiggle

Supposedly, a hundred-foot-tall Bellsprout once served as the main support pillar during the construction of Sprout Tower in Violet City. Similar to the body of a Bellsprout, the pillar inside the tower constantly sways back and forth, allowing earthquakes to be cushioned. This technology also exists in the real world and is used to construct modern skyscrapers.

## Hi, What's Your Name?

The name of a Pokémon differs from language to language; after all, the monster should have a name that sounds as natural and appropriate as possible. To achieve this, translators submit a series of name suggestions and the corresponding explanations to a committee of Pokémon Company executives. A name can't be random; it has to have a connection to the Pokémon. Squirtle, for example, already sounds like turtle. While names in early evolutionary stages should sound cute, names in later evolutions focus on coolness and strength. This is very important: The name of a Pokémon must not have a negative meaning in another language.

## Short & Sweet

Pokémon as a zodiac? The Unova horoscope makes it possible! There, different Pocket Monsters represent the zodiac signs from the real world: Bouffalant, for example, symbolizes the constellation Taurus, and Scolipede, Scorpio.

The Electric-Ghost Rotom has six different forms depending on the device it occupies. Interestingly, each shape was created by another designer – only the basic version was penned by Pokémon veteran Ken Sugimori.

When the talking Pikachu is tickled in a scene in the movie *Detective Pikachu*, it says the phrase "Sweet Mother of Arceus" instead of "Holy Mother of God." This is the first time the word "God" is replaced with the name of the god of the Pokémon universe, Arceus.

# The Most Important Thing: Berries

Shuckle is undoubtedly a special Pokémon. For instance, its base attack and HP stats are among the lowest of all known monsters. But it has the highest defense of all Pokémon that can be caught in a normal way due to the stable shell of the turtle. Inside, Shuckle collects berries and ferments them to create the infamous berry juice, which can be used to make a love potion.

## Pikachu to Go

Pokémon Pikachu – Nintendo released a Tamagotchi-like device under this plain name in the late 1990s. In addition to a watch and a pedometer, it includes a virtual Pikachu that can be fed with collected watts. The successor appeared in the US in 2000 under the name Pokémon Pikachu Color with additional functions. One allows transferring items to the Game Boy Color via infrared – as long as a *Gold*, *Silver*, or *Crystal* version is inserted. Nintendo revived the idea of a pedometer; the remakes, *Pokémon HeartGold* and *SoulSilver*, accompanied the Pokéwalker. Players could collect steps en route and transfer them as experience points to the games.

## Secret Card

The first trading card to be first released not in Japan but internationally was the Dark Raichu card. It was designed by the franchise's card manufacturer at the time, Wizards of the Coast. Dark Raichu is also the first secret card ever, part of the *Team Rocket* expansion, where it is listed with the number 83/82. In Japan, however, it is part of the *Neo Revelation* expansion.

## The Rare Magikarp

After the photo safari *Pokémon Snap* was released for the N64 in Japan in 1999, a photo contest was also held in the Pocket Monsters' country of origin. The ten winners received 20 trading cards with their winning photos as the motif. However, since each individual received 20 cards of their motif, few winning pieces circulated. In March 2022, such a card with a Magikarp illustration surprisingly appeared at a Japanese auction. The scarce specimen fetched about 136,000 dollars. It is unknown where the other 19 Magikarp trading cards are located.

**In the main games of the Pokémon series, there is always a current-generation Nintendo console in the player's room.**

## An Inglorious Champ

Even a Pokémon Champion can lose his hard-earned title, and Spain's Rubén Puig Lecegui had to experience that firsthand. He won the 2012 *Pokémon Video Game Championships* in England. Afterward, however, the Spanish team celebrated more than boisterously. Feces were spread in the hotel hallway, and vandalism was committed. Neither the hotel staff nor the police were thrilled about this. Equally appalled was The Pokémon Company International, the organizer of the tournament. Considering their intended family-friendly climate, such behavior was unacceptable. As a result, the Champion was stripped of his title.

## Gray Version?

This was a novelty after 16 years of Pokémon history: When the *Black 2* and *White 2* versions were released in 2012, it was the first time that games in the core Pokémon series had a number in their name. They are direct successors to the *Black* and *White* versions. Thus, for the first time, no special version appeared, which was still standard in previous generations, such as *Pokémon Platinum* as a supplement to the *Pearl* and *Diamond* versions.

## A Lot of Swirl

Who would have thought Satoshi Tajiri's favorite Pokémon was not a bug? Insects may have inspired the Pokémon creator's idea for the Pocket Monsters. Still, the tadpole Poliwag takes first place on his personal ranking. Tajiri is particularly enthusiastic about the swirl on the Pokémon's belly, which represents its internal organs – just like real tadpoles.

## At Second Glance

The transform Pokémon Ditto is known for not being recognizable at first glance, which is particularly evident in the collectible card game. In the *Pokémon GO* set, certain Pocket Monsters are marked with a small Ditto icon, which has an unusual meaning. The cards have a sticker layer that you can peel off. If you peel the sticker off the card, its true nature is revealed. It is in fact Ditto, which has hidden its true identity under the sticker. According to the official rulebook, these cards must always be played as Ditto, and the stats on the sticker layer are invalid.

## From the Game Boy to the TV

What an impact! The first scenes of the Pokémon anime start with a fight between a Gengar and a Nidorino – just like the intro of the Japan-exclusive Game Boy games *Pokémon Red* and *Green*. This fight has been re-animated one-to-one, and even the Game Boy-typical sound effects and music have been adopted. After transitioning to anime style, the fight turns out to be a duel between two trainers in the Pokémon League, which Ash is watching on TV. The silhouette of one trainer suggests that he could be the Elite Four trainer Bruno. After Nidorino is defeated, he uses Onix, a Rock and Ground Pokémon, respectively, which is typical of the video game counterpart. It's also fitting that the Elite Four in the games make up the Pokémon League.

By the way, in the technically revised versions of the first game generation, which was also released in the US in September 1998, the intro appears in precisely the same way – at least in the *Red Version*. In *Pokémon Blue*, the Ghost monster Gengar fights a Jigglypuff instead of a Nidorino.

## Short & Sweet

With its evolution into Dragonite, the largest non-legendary Dragon Pokémon, Dragonair shrinks quite a lot – from 13'01" to 7'03".

*Pokkén Tournament* was the last Pokémon game for the Nintendo Wii U and the first title of the monster series for the Switch.

Does a Pokémon's Pokédex number have a specific meaning? Not really, because the entry number is primarily based on progress in the games. The lower the Pokédex number, the earlier the player tends to encounter that monster in their adventure.

## Giants in the Pokémon Realm

The largest fully developed form of a starter Pokémon is the Grass snake Serperior, at about 10'10". On the other end, the Fire monkey Infernape – with a height of about 3'11", is a true dwarf among the starters. If you look at the scales, the Fire rabbit Cinderace weighs the least at 72.8 lb. The Grass turtle Torterra, on the other hand, weighs in at 683.4 lb.

## Dangerous Machines

Are the machines broken? That's probably what European players of *Pokémon Platinum* thought when they first entered the Game Corner in Veilstone City. Due to stricter gambling regulations and, thus, increased age ratings from the European PEGI, Nintendo decided to replace the slot machines in the *Platinum Version* with simple coin dispensers. For the 3DS releases of *Pokémon Red*, *Blue*, and *Yellow*, they didn't go to the trouble and kept the slot machines. As a result, the games were given the "12+" PEGI label.

## Monster from Outer Space

A family from the US state of Kentucky claimed to have experienced a group of aliens attacking their house on their farmland in August 1955. The unknown figures were small, with dark skin, pointed ears, and light eyes. The incident probably inspired the developer Game Freak to design the Dark-Ghost Pokémon Sableye. By the way, the critters from the so-called Kelly Hopkinsville event were probably just a group of Virginia owls.

## A Stressful Job

The novels that Takeshi Shudo wrote at the end of the 1990s to accompany the Pokémon anime contain some exciting background information on the subject of Gym Leaders. The job is said to be a rather thankless one. Maintaining a Gym is expensive and pays only a small salary. In addition, if you are defeated three times in a row as a leader, your Gym loses its Pokémon League license. No wonder Brock and Misty would rather accompany Ash on his travels than take care of their Gyms.

# Short & Sweet

Photographer Tracey accompanies Ash on his trip to the Orange Islands and is the only one of Ash's close friends with an official last name. His full name is Tracey Sketchit.

Weird and cool – that's how the lead designer of the first Pokémon generations, Ken Sugimori, describes his favorite Pocket Monster, Gengar. Moreover, the famous ghost is easy to draw and comes from his pen, Sugimori admitted with amusement in an interview.

*Pokémon XD: Gale of Darkness* – that was the name of one of the last games released for the Nintendo GameCube. XD stands for "Extra Dimension."

## Bill the Genius

Although Bill, the inventor of the Pokémon Storage System in the first generations, lives and researches on Route 25 in the northern part of the Kanto region, he is actually from Goldenrod City in Johto. He still has a house there, where some of his family members live. Additionally, his grandfather lives in Fuchsia City. In nearby Celadone City, Bill studied at an elite university. What makes it special: Only elementary school-aged prodigies are enrolled at Celadone University.

## Heroes in the Making

What criteria should the starter Pokémon meet? Usually, the trio comprises Grass, Fire, and Water representatives. They must resemble recognizable animals. Also, the starters should not resemble any existing Pokémon too much. Finally, their respective type must match their animal role model and still look cute initially so the design can gain strength through the evolutions. Additionally, the starters are designed according to the characteristics of coolness, seriousness, and wit. Using the fifth-generation starters as an example, Snivy is cool, Oshawott is serious, and Tepig is witty.

## Pokémon Town

The citizens of the capital of the US state of Kansas felt the Pokémon hype in a special way in August 1998. The reason: The mayor of the city of Topeka renamed it "ToPikachu" for one day. This unusual promotional action was intended to promote the first-generation Game Boy games and the Pokémon anime. These were released in the US a month later, in September 1998. About 20 years later, the city was again allowed to call itself "ToPikachu" for a day. In October 2018, the repeated action promoted remakes of the first-generation *Pokémon: Let's Go*, Pikachu! and *Pokémon: Let's Go, Eevee!.*

## Down Below

A mystery of the Pokémon world: Does the mole monster Diglett have lower body parts? At least it's always shown with only its head sticking out of the ground. But there are signs of a possible lower body. For example, in the games, Diglett can learn the attacks Scratch and Slash, which would require some form of claws. Also, in the *Pokémon Mystery Dungeon: Red Rescue Team* and *Blue Rescue Team* games and their remake, a Diglett mentions that it has legs. Its companion Pokémon react to this in visible surprise. So it remains a mystery for now.

## Walk for Money

It has been hard to stop. Less than six years after the release of *Pokémon GO*, the mobile app has generated over six billion dollars in revenue. Players in the USA and Japan are responsible for the biggest profits.

## Shattered Dreams

The anime's former head story writer, Takeshi Shudo, has written a novel to accompany the anime, which partly goes into the backgrounds of some characters. According to the novel, Ash's mother, Delia, runs the only restaurant in Pallet Town. She always wanted to be a model, but she gave up on that dream to raise Ash and continue running the family restaurant.

## From Old to New

The design of the turtle Tirtouga might look familiar to some long-established Pokémon fans. In April 1997, a drawing of a turtle monster appeared in an issue of the *MicroGroup Game Review* magazine that didn't make it into the second-generation games, which were in development at the time. It wasn't until the fifth generation that the design was picked up again with Tirtouga.

## The Dark Side

In the Pokémon trading card game, a few cards represent a Professor Oak lookalike who works for the sinister Team Rocket. Fake Oak also appears in other media. In the manga, a Kadabra poses as a professor with the help of its Psy powers. And in several episodes of the anime, James from Team Rocket has pretended to be Professor Oak.

## More Than Strong

With the help of the Mega Stone, some monsters have had Mega Evolution capability since the sixth generation. This is limited to the battle time, as the mega-evolved monsters are powerful. Although the feature is extremely popular among fans, *Pokémon Sword* and *Shield* did not include it. 46 Pokémon can Mega Evolve, but 48 Mega Evolutions exist in total. Charizard and Mewtwo have two different forms, depending on their Mega Stone.

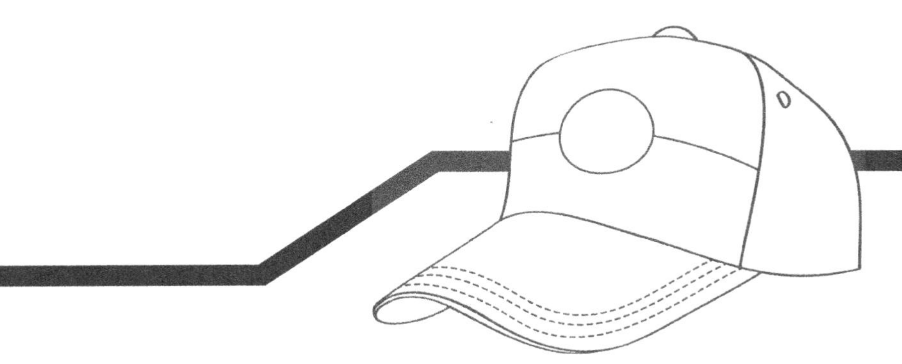

**When the designer of Pikachu, Atsuko Nishida, was asked about her favorite Pokémon, she named a not-so-cute Pocket Monster.**

**Her choice falls on the Fire dragon Charizard, also designed by her.**

## Old but Gold

There are ruins of ancient civilizations in the Kanto region. Near Pewter City, there was once the city of Pokélantis. After its king tried to achieve world domination with the help of Ho-Oh's powers, the legendary bird destroyed the city. Near Pallet Town once lay Pokémopolis. In its ruins, Ash and his friends discovered ancient artifacts that freed the giant monsters Gengar and Alakazam. Their size is unusual, and their tattoo-like decorations are striking. Anime fans shouldn't expect any references to these ancient cities in the games, though. After all, even though the alternate giant monster forms were well-received by viewers, they were never picked up in the games.

## Impact and Tread Resistant

Fists and legs fly when the Fighting Pokémon Hitmonchan and Hitmonlee enter the boxing ring. The boxing and kickboxing monsters are known for these moves. If you read their names carefully, you should notice something familiar. Hitmonchan is made up of the word "to hit" and the last name of the actor and martial arts star Jackie Chan. Hitmonlee also owes its name to the same English verb and the martial arts star and actor Bruce Lee.

## Short & Sweet

Isn't there something missing? If you take all the starter Pokémon and their evolutions, as well as their regional forms and Mega Evolutions from the main games together, almost all types are represented – only the types Ice, Rock, and Bug have not been considered yet.

XD001 – behind this codename is the Shadow Lugia corrupted by Cipher. Unlike other Shadow Pokémon, Lugia's transformation has also greatly changed its appearance.

No other type is as popular among the Elite Four as Ghost. By the seventh generation of the game, four elite trainers – Agatha, Phoebe, Shauntal, and Acerola – specialize in the Ghost-type, so they could theoretically start their own Pokémon League.

## Short & Sweet

In the anime, the Rock Pokémon Larvitar keeps Ash and his friends company for a certain period. The protagonist regularly carries the distrustful dinosaur monster in his arms – a mature achievement since, according to the Pokédex, Larvitar weighs around 159 lb.

The duck Farfetch'd almost became extinct. The reason is simple: Their meat, combined with the leek, which they always carry around, is considered a special treat.

Jessie's mother, Miyamoto, is a Team Rocket legend and has a simple guiding principle: One – profit, two – economize, no three or four, five – Pokémon! This makes her the ideal Team Rocket member.

## Loose Screw

Although they were introduced during the seventh generation of the game, the metallic nut Pokémon Meltan and its evolution do not appear in the Alola Pokédex. So far, it can only be caught in the *Pokémon GO* app and can only be evolved into Melmetal there. It can be transferred to other games via the *Pokémon Home* app or the Nintendo Switch games *Let's Go, Pikachu!* and *Let's Go, Eevee!*.

## Make One Out of Two

The Galaxy Expedition Team of the Hisui region led to the infamous Team Galactic, the Sinnoh region's crime organization. This is evident from their similar logos; moreover, they operate in the same area. Another clue is that in the Japanese original, no name distinction exists between the two groups. There, the expedition is also called Team Galactic.

## One for Me, Please!

Pocket Monsters from vending machines – it's possible! In Japan, these are called "Pokémon Stands" and mainly contain stuffed animals from the official Pokémon Stores. A few machines can also be found in various shopping malls in Seattle – not far from the headquarters of The Pokémon Company International. Other devices, from which you can only purchase trading cards, are located in the USA and South Korea.

## Take a Look Back

The Pokémon designs in some early trading cards don't quite match the design of their backgrounds. While the Pocket Monsters are based on iconic drawings, some of the locations are edited photos. For example, a Ponyta stands on a real meadow or a Wartortle on a real beach. The images for the backgrounds were not specially created. Some of them are still available on Japanese internet sites for stock images (i.e., pre-produced images that anyone can purchase).

## More Important Things Exist

Job or Snorlax? This dilemma was faced by two American police officers in April 2017. They were called to a robbery, but instead of doing their job, they preferred to play the mobile game *Pokémon GO*. This allowed them to capture the rare monsters Snorlax and Togetic, but not the robbers. However, their superiors did not find this funny and relieved the two officers of their duties.

## From Legend to Mystery

For a long time, Pokémon fans did not know mysterious monsters. Until the fifth generation, there was no distinction between them and the Legendaries. Since then, however, a separation has taken place. Mysterious Pokémon are characterized by their particular rarity, so their existence is even doubted by some in the Pokémon world. In the early games, they are not obtained in a common way but usually only through events. Examples are creatures like Mew or Shaymin.

## The Appearance of a Legend

The Pokémon's first anime episode already had a forward-looking surprise when it first aired. At the end of the episode, Ash spots an unknown flying creature in the sky: The legendary phoenix Pokémon Ho-Oh.

This appearance is special because the firebird belongs to the second generation and, thus, not to the first 151 Pokémon. Yet, it appears so early in the story. The episode debuted in Japan on April 1, 1997; thus, Ho-Oh debuted two and a half years before the *Gold* and *Silver* versions were released. The legendary phoenix even graces the cover of the Game Boy game *Pokémon Gold.* It is also the first legendary Pocket Monster to appear in the course of the anime – if you exclude the opening scenes – despite not appearing in the first-generation games.

Although Ho-Oh was revealed as early as August 1996 as part of the *Pokémon Silver* and *Gold* announcement in the Japanese magazine *CoroCoro Comic*, its appearance in the anime had fans worldwide going crazy with anticipation for the follow-up games.

## Yes or No?

Meowth hates water, right? You might think so; after all, he is a cat Pokémon. Indeed, his awe of water is regularly highlighted in the anime. However, Meowth jumps into the water at least as often. When he relaxes in a hot spring in one episode or goes swimming with pirates in another.

## A Colorful Mixture

With 18 different shapes, the butterfly Vivillon is a true master of diversity. Depending on where you start a new game in the real world, Vivillon appears in a different form. American players will see four different patterns, depending on their location. In contrast, in most areas of Japan, the butterfly will have an elegant pattern.

## Only With You

The two Pokémon, Karrablast and Shelmet, probably have one of the most unusual evolution methods. They evolve only when they are traded for each other. This is a unique case because no other Pocket Monsters must be traded for each other to evolve.

## Slightly Different Working Hours

Nine to five, as if! Pokémon creator Satoshi Tajiri seemingly has a problem with the usual working hours. Instead, he prefers to work 24 hours at a stretch. After a twelve-hour nap, he regains his strength and works for another full day. According to his statements, this unusual rhythm gives him the best game ideas.

## Not Child-Friendly

Some Pocket Monsters put a good face on the bad game. The Ghost balloon Pokémon Drifloon is one of them. It looks cute and innocent, but the Pokédex reveals its true nature. Drifloon makes children disappear. It grabs their hands and carries the children off into the afterlife. Drifloon's balloon-like body is made of stray souls, so when it bursts, the souls inside it escape with a scream.

## Not Welcome

In China, the Pokémon anime has not only fans but also a high-ranking enemy – much to the chagrin of Pokémon fans. Since September 2006, the Chinese government has restricted TV broadcasting between 5 and 8 p.m. This restriction was also extended by an hour in 2008. This is to promote Chinese animation studios by prohibiting the broadcast of foreign productions during this time. Accordingly, it's not just the Japanese production Pokémon that is affected.

## The Monster That Never Was

Initially, the Pokémon mascot Pikachu was supposed to have another evolution after Raichu, which even got a name: Gorochu. While there are no official drawings, in an interview, Pikachu creator Atsuko Nishida described Gorochu as a "god of thunder with claws and horns." To make the games more balanced, it was dropped – and Pikachu was given a predecessor in the second generation with Pichu.

## Short & Sweet

Each real-world Pokémon Center store has its own logo with different Pocket Monsters. The Hiroshima store logo even features a Shiny Pokémon: The red Gyarados.

To mark the 23rd anniversary of the first Pokémon movie, *Super Smash Bros.* creator Masahiro Sakurai tweeted a recreated image of the scene where Pikachu's clone slaps Pikachu. Sakurai's comment on it: Just thinking about that scene makes him cry.

According to Pokédex entries for the *Ultra Sun* and *Ultra Moon* versions, the virtual monster Porygon was created by scientists about 20 years earlier. This is a reference to the first Pokémon games, *Red* and *Green*, which were released 20 years earlier.

## Not Cute Enough

Why so evil? Early in the development of *Pokémon Red* and *Green*, head designer Ken Sugimori was responsible for most of the monster designs. But his creations mostly looked vicious or tough. For a closer emotional connection with the player, however, cute Pokémon were also needed. Sugimori managed only one cute creation: Clefairy. Game Freak then tried to hire a female designer and found one in Atsuko Nishida. She was the first female employee at Game Freak and the fourth member of the design team.

Her employment fully paid off, as Nishida then designed not only the iconic Pokémon mascot Pikachu but also popular, cute monsters like the starters Bulbasaur, Squirtle, and Charmander. But Nishida could do more than just cute; tough-acting fan favorites like Charizard and Zoroark were also designed by Game Freak's first female employee. Whether a Pokémon is ultimately cute enough is decided by Snorlax's role model, Koji Nishino. The game designer was appointed "Cuteness Supervisor" within Game Freak. Thus, Pokémon designs are made cuter or signed off as cute enough on his instructions.

## Accompanied by Your Partner Pikachu

*Pokémon Yellow* owners can admire their yellow favorite in very special action in *Pokémon Stadium* for the N64. If you connect the Game Boy cartridge to *Pokémon Stadium* via the N64 Transfer Pak, Pikachu can enter the battle stadium. Unlike a Pikachu that is not loaded into the game via the *Yellow Version*, the personal electric mouse calls its name with its familiar voice from the anime. Its animations also distinguish it from other representatives of its species.

## Make Rocket Great Again!

The last Pokémon title released for the Game Boy Color is the Japan-exclusive sequel to *Pokémon Trading Card Game*. Part two bears the loosely translated subtitle *Here Comes Team GR!* which refers to the crime syndicate Team Great Rocket. The organization kidnaps the club masters of the predecessor and captures TCG Island. The game came with the exclusive promo cards Great Rocket Mewtwo and Great Rocket Lugia.

# Short & Sweet

The mushroom Pokémon Foongus and its evolution Amoonguss imitate the appearance of a Poké Ball with their pattern. Their Shiny variants feature the coloring of a Master Ball.

When *Pokémon X* and *Y* were released in October 2013, the two legendary monsters Xerneas and Yveltal graced the cover of the Nintendo 3DS games. Fittingly, they were specially designed in the shape of the corresponding letters.

At around 150 million dollars, *Detective Pikachu* is the Pokémon movie with the highest production budget. At the same time, no other movie from the Pokémon universe made as much money: *Detective Pikachu* earned over 433 million US dollars into the world's box offices.

## Change of Heart

Jessie and James don't just have Ash and his friends as enemies. In fact, their true archenemies are Butch and Cassidy – a successful Team Rocket duo who have already trumped their achievements in Team Rocket Academy. Butch and Cassidy's efforts were always recognized by Giovanni, yet they turned their backs on the criminal organization to open a bakery together in a small coastal village. By the way, their namesake was the American outlaw Butch Cassidy.

## The Only One of Its Kind

Takeshi Shudo is the only person who was not employed by the Pokémon developer, Game Freak, and yet created a Pocket Monster. He was the lead story writer for the Pokémon anime until 2002. During the second anime film's production, he invented the legendary creature Lugia, around which the film's story revolves. To Shudo's surprise, Lugia was so well-received by Game Freak that it promptly graced the cover of *Pokémon Silver* and continued to appear in the video games. Thus, Lugia is the only Pokémon not designed by Game Freak.

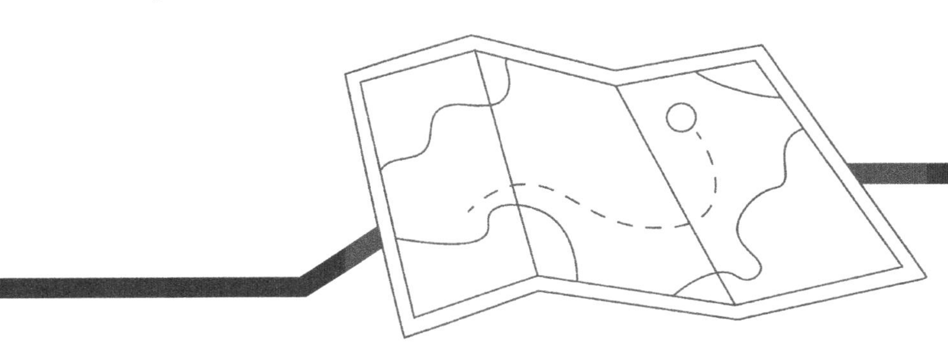

**Although legendary Pokémon can't reproduce, the N64 photo shooting game Pokémon Snap features the legendary birds Articuno, Zapdos, and Moltres hatching from eggs.**

Made in the USA
Monee, IL
02 February 2024

52850390R00105